The
GREAT
Commission
Challenge

Christian Heritage Publication
An Imprint of:
Great Commission Incorporation
7 Enmore Road
South Norwood
London
SE25 5NQ
United Kingdom

Scripture quotations are taken from:
King James (KJV) Bible © Crown Copyright
New King James (NKJV) Bible © 1982 by Thomas Nelson Inc
New International Version (NIV) Bible
Used by permission. All rights reserved

ISBN: 978-0-9570933-7-9

Cover design by Imoh Ussenudoh (imoh@me.com)
Editorial Work by Mrs Nana Fosua Babatunde (nakuafosua@outlook.com)

Dedication

I dedicate this book to my father, Elder Joshua Oluboboye Babatunde, who God used by divine providence to lay the foundation of my Christian faith. The first seeds of missions, world-evangelism and my love for hymns were sown both at home and at my first church – Surulere Baptist Church, under the Pastorate of the Late Rev. S. O. Daramola. For the tremendous impact you've had in my life and calling as a servant of God, I am immensely grateful. Thank you, Daddy, and may God reward you both here and in the life to come!

Contents

Acknowledgements

Relationships are key to life as no man is an island. One's purpose or destiny would never be fulfilled without the input and contri-butions of strategic persons. I have been blessed by God to have benefited immensely from such relationships.

This book would never have seen the light of day, but for the help, contributions and deposits made into my life! If I try to re-member everyone who has impacted me in one way or the other over the last five decades and more, my memory would fail me.

I, however, want to express my appreciation to the following: all my mentors, pastors, spiritual guides and counsellors, teachers and instructors, who have poured into my life, what God has graced them with. To my World Harvest Christian Centre family worldwide, thank you for supporting, encouraging and praying for me always.

My special thanks go out to the Babatunde clan; like Timothy in the Scriptures, a lot of the things I enjoy today are the result of the rich spiritual heritage I inherited from the Babatundes.

I am eternally indebted to my immediate family - my biological children and my wife, Nana Fosua, for their unconditional love, support, and enormous sacrifice, which has allowed me to answer the call of God.

To the thrice Holy God be the glory, honour and adoration!

Foreword

We live in challenging times, where to some degree, the advance-ment of human knowledge, skills and technology can provide remedies for some of humanity's challenges.

However, there remain issues that cannot be resolved without Divine Intervention. This need for the active workings of the authority and power given to the Church, as a means of solving the humanly unsolvable, has attracted many to the Church as a solution centre and a place of "covering".

While the Church in that sense is a great blessing to many and a bastion of hope to the despairing, there lurks the danger of ignoring the Great Commission of the Lord which is primarily, the soul-winning, disciple-making mandate of the Church.

This mandate is:

To Go

To Teach

To Baptise and

To Command Obedience.

Matthew 28:18-20:

"And Jesus came and spake unto them, saying, 'All power is given unto me in heaven and in earth.

Go ye therefore, and teach all nations, baptizing them in the name

of the Father, and of the Son, and of the Holy Ghost: Teaching
them to observe all things whatsoever I have commanded you: and,
lo, I am with you alway, even unto the end of the world.'" Amen
(KJV)

Addressing the danger of overlooking this alpha mandate of the
Body of Christ, as well as enlisting and equipping end-time har-
vesters, is the driving inspiration of the author of "The Great
Commission Challenge".

Wale Babatunde is an end-time revivalist with a passionate cry
to the Church to rise up from the culture of self-centeredness,
which has permeated most of what is preached from pulpits
across the nations and dominated the mind of the Body of Christ.

With soul-wrenching urgency, he sounds a clarion call to rouse
labourers and harvesters to the task and stewardship entrusted to the
Church by its Lord - to be the instrument of God for the
proclamation of the Gospel of Jesus Christ and His Kingdom.

With earnestness and fervency of spirit, he reminds the Church
of both eternal rewards for the faithful discharge of our divine
duty and the consequences of neglecting the oracles of God entrusted to us for the end-time harvest.

In his book "The Great Commission Challenge", Wale Babatunde begins by stirring the heart of the reader and igniting a
"fire in the bones" experience that cannot be ignored.

"Then I said, I will not make mention of him, nor speak any
more in his name. But his word was in mine heart as a burning
fire shut up in my bones, and I was weary with forbearing, and I
could not stay." (Jeremiah 20:9; KJV)

With insights for operational evangelism, he skilfully navi-
gates, equips and empowers the reader with dynamic keys and
modes for effective soul winning, spanning from methodologies

for fruitful evangelism to the supernatural dimensions of the Great Commission.

This book, one among several written by Wale Babatunde, is a must-read for believers who have lost their fire for the divine assignment, have gone into a state of spiritual apathy and yearn to get back their passion for the Gospel, its proclamations and its amazing impact.

"The Great Commission Challenge" will compel you to seek and receive a fresh impartation of divine boldness and a re-activation of dormant gifts for Kingdom operations.

This book will not only trigger a revivalist spirit in you, but will also motivate you to step out of your comfort zone, pick up the baton of what has been passed down to us by the Apostolic Fa-thers, and walk in the power and rewards of God's soul-winners.

May posterity say of you in the words of the Apostle Paul, that you were "not disobedient unto the heavenly vision" - Acts 26:19.

"The Great Commission Challenge" is an indispensable book

that will challenge your witness for these challenging times.

Archbishop Nicholas Duncan Williams

General Overseer, Action Chapel International,

Ghana

Endorsement I

The author delivers the ultimate mandate given by God to man in an unabashed manner. The references to real-life incidents, indeed, bring clarity and purpose to this message. It reaches out to a large section of the saved and yet to be saved souls with its credibility based on the teachings of Christ.

Rev. Wale Babatunde takes readers on a journey of discovery of the Truth and leaves them yearning to share this knowledge, and in the process, fulfil the Great Commission that has been given to each one of us.

My congratulations to Rev. Wale Babatunde for bringing out this exhaustive text which readers can use as a tool for furthering the real cause of believers.

Rev. D. Mohan
General Superintendent – Assemblies of God International
Senior Pastor – New Life Assemblies of God Church
Chennai, India

Endorsement II

Indeed, we are not just in the last days but the very last of the last days. My brother and co -labourer, Pastor Wale Babatunde, speaks along the same lines in this wake-up epistle to the Church of Christ. He says, "We are living on borrowed time. These are not just the last days, they are the very last seconds of the last days." It is a clarion call to all stakeholders to buy into the move of the Spirit, to restructure the Church and the work of the ministry. The Church should be seen beyond the four walls of our buildings and taken to the highways and byways as this is the desire of the Father.

While soul winning is the heartbeat of Abba Father, it is disturbing to see His children display a lackadaisical attitude towards it.

In two of the most dramatic conversions to ever occur in Scripture - Zacchaeus the tax collector and the Samaritan woman, Jesus uttered His mission statement in words that baffled His hearers. He said, "…The Son of man is come to seek and to save that which was lost" (Luke 19:10; KJV). And in John 4:34, He said, "…My meat is to do the will of Him that sent Me, and to finish His work" (KJV).

There has never been greater urgency in Heaven than there is now for the earth to see the manifestation of the Sons of God. It is time for us, sons on earth, to put in the sickle and reap the ripe harvest. Let us be the wise sons who gather fruit in summer (Proverbs 10:5). We have been chosen to bear much fruit in our union with the Father and the Son by the power of the Holy Spirit (John 15:1-8, 16).

Truth be told, we are the eleventh-hour labourers who have come into the harvest of the labour of our heroes past (Matthew 20:1-6; John 4:34-38). Time has been given to us to prepare for eternity. Let us, therefore, heighten our commitment to bear trophies before our soon-coming King. What a delight it will be for the King to see us with the prizes of the great price He paid at the Cross. Let us live our lives on earth for that day in Heaven when we shall hear Him say,

> "Well done, thou good and faithful servant... enter thou into the joy of thy Lord."
> (Matthew 25:21; KJV)

Let's accept The Great Commission Challenge and rush into the end-time harvest of souls. This timely book will not only challenge you but also offers very helpful guidelines that will greatly bless your resolve to heed the Master's call. I recommend it for all Ministers, church workers and all serious believers.

Apostle Goodheart O. Ekwueme
Lead Pastor, RHOGIC
Abuja, Nigeria

Introduction

For almost three and a half decades, God has placed a singular burden on my heart - which is to see the whole Church of Christ rise to the challenge of the Great Commission. It is over two thousand years now since we were first given the marching orders by our Commander. If there was a time that believers must become desperate for the souls of men, it is now! Today, as all Biblical prophecies about the end times are being fulfilled before our very eyes, the divine clock is on a countdown!

As those who passionately love the King and His Kingdom, we must be preparing what we would present to Him at His coronation. Nothing would be more fitting than offering the Lamb the reward of His sacrifice - Souls! This is the hour for all believers to invest their time, talents and treasures in what matters to God most. Is there any motivation for us to give our best and all? Yes, indeed! Christ has promised the soul winner a Crown of Rejoicing. We must, therefore, unleash everything in our arse-nal - prayer, healing, miracles, signs and wonders, to bring in the ripened harvest of the world.

Like Esther, God has raised us up at this strategic hour, and blessed us with resources like no other generation before us; for we have been raised for such a time as this! We must arise for the salvation of the multitudes trooping into a Christless eternity.

The baton has been handed over to us by our forebears who have now joined the cloud of witnesses, cheering us on to awake out of slumber, apathy and indifference and complete the Great

Commission in our generation. The Big question for us then is - will we, the Church, respond to this challenge?

CHAPTER 1

ARE YOU DESPERATE FOR SOULS?

"I believe that in each generation God has called enough men and women to evangelize all the yet unreached tribes of the earth. It is not God who does not call - it is man who will not respond." - Isobel Kuhn

"We must be global Christians with a global vision because our God is a global God."
- John R. W. Stott

"Satan is so much more in earnest than we are - he buys up the opportunity while we are wondering how much it will cost." - Amy Carmichael

"Lost people matter to God and so they must matter to us." - Keith Wright

"Sympathy is no substitute for action."
- David Livingstone

How true the saying is - "your attitude will always determine your altitude." Attitudes are the major determinants of how successful a person will be. I have studied the lives of a few men and women - both in the secular as well as in sacred history. They had one thing in common: they were never half-hearted in their desire to be successful or excel in life. These men and women were never going to accept 'no' for an answer when it came to the pursuit of excellence. They were prepared to sacrifice anything, includ-ing their very lives, to attain great heights. Nothing was going to stand in their way. No matter how many times they fell or failed, they were never going to give up.

I have watched the children of this generation do everything: give up pleasures, food, sleep, leisure, and other things, to become athletic, boxing, or football champions. They also refuse to give up until they've achieved their dreams! Thomas Alva Edison, one of America's greatest inventors made 1,000 unsuccessful attempts before inventing the light bulb. What if he gave up? When a re-porter asked, "How did it feel to fail 1,000 times?", Edison replied, "I didn't fail 1,000 times - the light bulb was an invention with 1,000 steps". This is the attitude world changers and history mak-ers have. This is what we need as Soul Winners.

Let's consider a few other men who never gave up:

Abraham Lincoln went to war a Captain and returned a Pri-vate. Afterwards, he was a failure as a businessman. As a law-yer in Springfield, he was too impractical and temperamental to be a success. He turned to politics and was defeated in his first try for the legislative, again defeated in his first application to be commissioner of the general land office, defeated in the senato-rial election of 1854, defeated in his effort for Vice Presidency in 1856, and defeated in the senatorial election of 1858. At about that time, he wrote in a letter to a friend, "I am now the most mis-erable man living". He eventually became the 16th president of the United States of America in March 1861. Any lessons? Never give up! Failure is never final!

Henry Ford was an American industrialist and business mag-nate. He founded the Ford Motor Company and was the sponsor of the development of the assembly line technique of mass pro-duction. Yet, he failed and went broke 5 times before he succeeded.

Rowland Hussey Macy was an American businessman who founded one of the largest and most successful retail businesses in the world. What most people are unaware of is the fact that he failed 7 times before his store in New York broke through.

Winston Churchill repeated a grade during elementary school, and when he entered Harrow, was placed in the lowest division of the lowest class. He later twice failed the entrance exam to the Royal Military Academy at Sandhurst. He was defeated in his first effort to serve in Parliament. At the age of 62, he became the Prime Minister of England. He later wrote, "Never give in, never give in, never, never, never, in nothing great or small, large or petty. Never give in except to convictions of honour and good sense. Never, Never, Never Give Up!"

Albert Einstein did not speak until he was 4 years old and did not read until he was 7. His parents thought he was "abnormal" and one of his teachers described him as mentally slow, unsociable and adrift, forever in foolish dreams. He was expelled from school and was refused admittance to the Zurich Polytechnic School, yet later on, developed the "Theory of Relativity" - one of the two pillars of modern physics.

My questions for your consideration and reflection are:

Why have we given up on soul winning, this lofty mandate from the Thrice Holy God?

Why have we allowed obstacles and what Paul calls "light afflic-tions" to stop us from reaping "the end-time harvest"?

Why, why, why have we been unfaithful in the Lord's service for

so many years? Always looking for excuses, ranging from "I am too busy" to "the ground is hard"!

I have tried my best to cover up for our nonchalant attitude but the truth is glaring. Many believers today cannot point to a single soul that they have won and discipled for the Lord.

Can I ask - how many Souls have you won in the last 1, 2, 3 or 5 years?

I have seen pastors, church elders, board members and even some so-called evangelists who do not know what it means to lead a soul to Calvary. How can we be pastors, evangelists, teach-ers, prophets or apostles without souls? If many church leaders, elders and board members were football coaches, with our per-formances, we would have been fired long ago. Of what use is fishing without catching, and planting without harvesting?

How desperate are you for souls? I know what we are desperate for – cars, houses, business contracts, visas to travel and to kill our household enemies!

In January of every year - many Christians fast, some for 7 days, others for 14, 21, 30, 40, 60, 70, and some even 100 days. What are our prayer points? Your guess is as good as mine - tem-poral things! Could I appeal to you that we add this important issue which is big on the heart of God – Soul Winning!

We will never win the world with our half-hearted attitude. Our neighbours, colleagues and the heathen will never be reached and converted until we become desperate!

Rachael, Jacob's favourite wife, was barren just as many of us are, yet she cried out of desperation, "...give me children, or else I die." - Genesis 30:1 (KJV)

Hannah refused to be comforted to the extent that her hus-band, Elkanah, said to her - "Am I not more than ten sons?" She refused to eat or to engage in any pleasurable activities un-til she became fruitful with the greatest prophet from Dan to

Beer-Sheba, Samuel (1 Samuel 1:8-20).

The Syro-Phoenician woman in Matthew 15:21-28, whose daughter was demon-possessed, was faced with several obstacles, including being ignored and insulted, but she was not perturbed until she got what she wanted. This woman was not only desper-ate but she would not give up!

John Knox was a desperate man. He wanted his nation at all cost to bow to the Lordship of Jesus. Check out his prayer - "Give me Scotland or I die". His ministry of preaching and prayer was so well known that Mary, Queen of Scots, whose government had persecuted Knox, is reported to have said: "I fear the prayers of John Knox more than all the assembled armies of Europe".

Paul, the Apostle, was a desperate Soul Winner. In Romans 9:1-3, he declared that he would be willing to trade-in his eternal salvation for that of his Jewish countrymen - "for I could wish that I myself were cursed and cut off from Christ for the sake of my brothers, those of my own race, the people of Israel" (NIV).

John 'Praying' Hyde, an American missionary to India, was so desperate to change the face of the country where he lived, along with the state of fruitlessness in his ministry. The prayers on his lips were, "Give me Souls - first, one a day, then two, then three, then four, then eight..."

Charles Cowman - It was said of the founder of the Oriental Missionary Society, who was a missionary evangelist to Japan, that the winning of a soul, was to him what the winning of a battle is to a soldier and a race to an athlete. He was said to live for only one thing - to win Souls for Christ, and his burden for Japan caused him to say - "By the help of God, they shall hear, even if it costs every drop of my life's blood". Heaven is filled with desperate soul winners. Will you be the next one?

CHAPTER 2

WHAT WILL YOU LAY AT JESUS' FEET?

"If Jesus Christ be God and died for me, then no sacrifice
can be too great for me to make for Him."
– Charles Thomas Studd

"People who do not know the Lord ask why in the world we waste our
lives… and when the bubble has burst, they will have nothing of
eternal significance to show for the years they have wasted." – Nate
Saint, Missionary Martyr

It was England's longest reigning monarch in history, Queen
Elizabeth I (1837-1901), who famously wished for Jesus' second
coming during her reign, so that she would be the first earthly
monarch to lay down her crown at His feet.

John, the revelator in the Apocalypse, on the Island of Patmos,
was given a glimpse of the throne of God where he saw the
living creatures and the twenty-four elders worship the Lamb.

He writes:

"Whenever the living creature give glory, honour and thanks to him who

sits on the throne and who lives for ever and ever, the twenty-four elders

fall down before him who sits on the throne and worship him who lives for

ever and ever. They lay their crowns before the throne and say: 'You

are worthy, our Lord and God to receive glory and honour and power, for you created all things, and by your will they were created and have their being.'"
– Revelation 4:9-11 (NIV)

Do you know that a day is coming when every knee will bow and every tongue confess that Jesus is Lord?! Are you aware that one day, you are going to see your Saviour face to face?! Have you ever considered what you would present to Him?! In our culture, when you are visiting someone that you hold in high esteem, you tend to go with precious gifts. When we visit earthly monarchs or potentates, we tend to take along the best gifts that money can buy. When Jesus was born, the wise men brought to Him precious gifts - gold, myrrh and frankincense. Have you thought of the gift that you will be presenting to King Jesus at His coronation?

Throughout the history of the Church, it has always been the most ardent lovers of Jesus who have felt the greatest need for more of His presence. Surely, it is of this class of saints that Count Nicolaus Ludwig Von Zinzendorf belongs. For Zinzendorf, lov-ing fellowship with Christ was the essential manifestation of the Christian life. Flowing out of Zinzendorf's passionate love for Christ, came a life of disciplined prayer. The Moravian prayer re-vival began in 1727 and lasted unbroken for 100 years; the longest prayer movement the world has ever known. The Moravian leader believed that the best antidote to a powerless Church was the influence of a praying man.

As Zinzendorf's passion for Jesus and prayer grew, so did his passion for the lost. He determined to evangelise the world with a handful of believers. The Moravian brotherhood readily received and perpetuated the passion of their leader. A seal was designed to express their newfound missionary zeal; it comprised a lamb on a crimson ground with the cross of resurrection and a banner of triumph with the motto: "our lamb has conquered, let us follow him."

On October 8, 1732, a Dutch ship left the Copenhagen harbour bound for the Danish West Indies. On board were the first two Moravian missionaries, John Leonard Dober, a potter, and David Nitschman, a carpenter. Both were skilled workers, ready to sell themselves into slavery to reach the slaves of the West Indies. As the ship slipped away, they lifted a cry that would one day become the rallying call for all Moravian Missionaries - "May the Lamb that was slain receive the reward of His suffering or sacrifice." To the Moravians, the greatest offering one can present to the Lord for His suffering and sacrifice is the souls of men. This was what motivated them to be one of the most outstanding missionary movement the world has known.

Friends, I know that you may be living in an exquisite, tasteful and expensive home. You might be driving a truly splendid, spiffy, speedy, flashy, gallant and gorgeous car. However, let it be known that no matter how expensive or beautiful our earthly possessions may be, we will not be able to present any of these to the Lamb of God. They will all pass away with this present world. There is nothing we count as being valuable on earth that will be worth anything once we cross over into eternity.

However, I know of something that will be well-pleasing to the Lord when it is presented to Him upon seeing Him face to face. I know of something when presented, will throw the whole of the angelic host into a frenzy. I know of something that you can present to the Lord that will earn you a great reward. I know of something that I am convinced about which will not only put a smile on Jesus' face but will also receive a resounding accolade of "well done, good and faithful servant".

Friend, if you invest in stocks and shares, you can get a fantastic reward. My brother and sister, you can invest in a business and become very rich like Bill Gates, Alakija or Dangote. However, remember, you will leave all these things on earth. "Naked you came, naked you will leave".

Invest in souls – And you will never regret it.

Pray for the salvation of souls – you will never regret

it. What will you present at the feet of Jesus? Nothing

can be better than the Souls of Men!

CHAPTER 3

DO YOU HAVE BLOOD ON YOUR HANDS?

"As long as there are millions destitute of the Word of God and knowledge of Jesus Christ, it will be impossible for me to devote time and
energy to those who have both."
– J. L. Ewen

"You have one business on earth - to save souls."
– John Wesley

"The church that does not evangelize will fossilize."
– Oswald J. Smith

"The Great Commission says to make disciples, not get followers.
There is a difference."
– Miguel Nunez

"Could a mariner sit idle if he heard the drowning cry? Could a doctor
sit in comfort and just let his patients die? Could the fireman sit idle,
let men burn and give no hand? Can you sit at ease in Zion with
the world around you damned?"
– Leonard Ravenhill

"The word of the LORD came to me: "Son of man, speak to your people and say to them: 'When I bring the sword against a land, and the people of the land choose one of their men and make him their watchman, and he sees the sword coming against the land and blows the trumpet to warn the people, then if anyone hears the trumpet but does not heed the warning and the sword comes and takes their life, their blood will be on their own head. Since they heard the sound of the trumpet but did not heed the warning, their blood will be on their own head. If they had heeded the warning, they would have saved themselves. But if the watchman sees the sword coming and does not blow the trumpet to warn the people and the sword comes and takes someone's life, that person's life will be taken because of their sin, but I will hold the watchman accountable for their blood.'" – Ezekiel 33:1-6 (NIV)

The above scripture is the Ministry of the Watchman! We find a similar description of the work of a Watchman in Ezekiel 3:16-19 (NIV):

"At the end of seven days the word of the LORD came to me: "Son of man, I have made you a watchman for the people of Israel; so hear the word I speak and give them warning from me. When I say to a wicked person, 'You will surely die,' and you do not warn them or speak out to dissuade them from their evil ways in order to save their life, that wicked person will die for their sin, and I will hold you accountable for their blood. But if you do warn the wicked person and they do not turn from their wickedness or from their evil ways, they will die for their sin; but you will have saved yourself."

Many Christians are heading home to Heaven, not fully aware of what might be waiting for them on the other side.

According to these two passages, God has committed an important responsibility into the hands of the watchman. First, God reveals to the watchman impending judgement, for which he is to blow the trumpet, warning the land about it. If he blows the trum-pet and warns the people but they refuse to heed the warning, his hands are clean and their blood will be on their heads. However, if the watchman refuses to warn the people - in other words, he keeps silent and the people are destroyed, God's Word states that the people's blood will be on the watchman's head and He will, one day, require their blood from his hands.

Do you think you would be commended for walking past your neighbour's house which was on fire without calling in the fire service? Certainly not! You would be seen as a very wicked person. Or what if you suddenly discovered the cure for cancer and you kept the information to yourself and several people whose lives could have been saved from the deadly disease died? If after some time, the community and the whole nation discovered the secret you kept from them, would you be celebrated? No! Many would consider your actions as wicked and inhumane.

Can I put it to you as a Christian who has received the knowl-edge of God's saving grace, Jesus Christ, that if you keep from your family, friends, colleagues, associates etc. the way of salvation - how they can be saved from the wrath to come, do you think you will escape? What about your brother, sister, spouse, uncle, grand-parent, in-laws and so on, whom you spend several hours, days, months, and years with, and you've never once opened your mouth to share the Good News of God's saving grace? Do you think God will commend you? I don't think so! You will make Heaven, but as you enter Heaven and open your hands, it will be filled with men's blood and God will hold you responsible for their blood.

Scriptures declare that by the mouth of two or more witnesses every truth shall be established. Proverbs 24:11–12 (NIV):

Rescue those being led away to death; hold back those staggering toward slaughter." "If you say, "But we knew nothing about this," does not he who weighs the heart perceive it? Does not he who guards your life know it? Will he not repay everyone according to what they have done?

In view of the terrifying judgment that awaits the unregenerate, let's learn from the chief of all Apostles, his modus operandi:

"Since, then, we know what it is to fear the Lord, we try to persuade men."
– 2 Corinthians 5:11 (NIV)

When last did you plead, beg, or appeal to your stubborn child about the judgement to come? Can you remember the last time you shed tears for your husband, daughter or son? Have you been on your knees lately?

Charlie Peace was a criminal in England, a man who neither feared man nor God! Soon, the laws of the land caught up with him and he was sentenced to die. On the eve of his execution, the priest led him on a death walk, reading the Scriptures almost half asleep, without any emotion regarding where this criminal was heading the next day. After some time, Charlie Peace asked the priest what he was reading. He replied - "Consolation of Religion". Charlie Peace then responded - "how could a man say that he believes in eternal damnation and yet a fellow human being was heading there in a matter of hours, yet be without emotion". His words to the priest were "if I believe what you Christians say you believe about hell-fire, if England was filled with broken bottles from coast to coast, I will go everywhere if need be on my knees pleading with men not to go to hell." This criminal's response is damning to most believers and preachers on how we handle the subject of eternal damnation. I am totally convinced that most church leaders don't believe or subscribe to the Biblical teachings on hell.

The Hippocratic Oath in our "Oath of Ethics", historically taken by physicians is one of the most widely known medical texts. It requires a new physician to swear by a number of healing gods to uphold specific ethical standards. One of the oaths they must swear and adhere to is to do everything within their power to save and rescue lives. Can we as Christians today, under God, take a similar oath to do everything within our power to deliver souls racing to a Christless eternity?

Someone once asked me, "why do you make altar calls after every message?" I am sure some of you must have been wondering, is it not a waste of time? Let me share with you one of the motivating reasons.

The great Chicago Fire began at about 9 p.m. on Sunday, October 8th, until early Tuesday, October 10th, 1871. This fire killed approximately 300 people. This fire greatly impacted the life and ministry of the famous 19th-century evangelist, D. L. Moody. He had held his usual service that fateful Sunday evening the fire broke out. At the close of the service, he asked his congregation to evaluate their relationship with Christ and return the follow-ing week to make a decision. This, he thought, would give them enough time to reflect on a lasting decision. Within a matter of hours, many of those who sat under his hearing were dead. Moody afterwards became very ill because of the guilt that consumed him - not knowing where most of his parishioners would spend eter-nity. He decided afterwards never to end another sermon without offering his listeners the opportunity to make a decision to give their lives to Christ.

The Scripture is clear regarding when God's acceptable time for salvation is:

"For he saith, I have heard thee in a time accepted, and in the day of salvation have I succoured thee: behold, now is the accepted time; behold, now is the day of salvation." – 2 Corinthians 6:2 (KJV)

CHAPTER 4

COUNTDOWN!

"The mission of the Church is to seek
and to save them that are lost." – James
H. Aughey

"God has given Believers the responsibility of spreading the
Gospel to all the world and we need to use all at our disposal to
accomplish this task."
– Theodore H. Epp

"To call a man evangelical who is not evangelistic
is an utter contradiction!"
– G. Campbell Morgan

"If you had the cure to cancer wouldn't you share it? ... If you
have the cure to death... get out there and share it."
– Kirk Cameron

"The end of all things is at hand."
– 1 Peter 4:7 (KJV)

Anyone who knows me intimately from my youth, living in La-gos,

Nigeria, will tell you that I have always played and loved the game of football. The time given for a competitive football match is 90 minutes. After 90 minutes, the referee has the prerogative to add on injury time. Once the full-time is exhausted, the football-ers know that they are on a countdown or borrowed time, which is usually only a few minutes. During this period, particularly if the match is competitive, footballers tend to exert all their energy and take certain risks that were not taken during the 90 minutes. It is common to see goalkeepers leave their goalposts for their opponent's post, to assist in scoring a goal. Some goalkeepers have been very fortunate to have scored during this additional time.

Nothing is as bad as being out of sync with spiritual timing. In my estimation, most believers are unaware of where we are on God's clock.

> "The Pharisees and Sadducees came to Jesus and tested him by asking him to show them a sign from heaven. He replied, "When evening comes, you say, 'It will be fair weather, for the sky is red,' and in the morning, 'Today it will be stormy, for the sky is red and overcast.' You know how to interpret the appearance of the sky, but you cannot in-terpret the signs of the times."
> – Matthew 16:1-3 (NIV)

In the above scripture, Jesus upbraided the spiritual elites of his days for being able to predict the weather accurately, but not being able to discern the times.

A man of God had a strange encounter. He was driving and suddenly saw a very old man by the roadside struggling. He decid-ed to give him a lift. As they drove off, the old man asked the man of God - "Do you know what happened yesterday in Heaven?" He was shocked that the old man would ask such a question. How could anyone know what transpired in Heaven without being an angel or one of the spiritual beings that are before the Throne of God? The old man continued – "Last night, the Father told the angels to get ready to blow the trumpet to herald the coming of His Son, Jesus Christ. Then Jesus appeared, pleading with the Father with tears, that if the angels blew the trumpet now, the Church is far from ready, and more so, His death on the cross would have been wasted for the millions or even billions of souls that He paid the price for their salvation." Suddenly, the old man disappeared and the man of God was persuaded that God allowed him to experience this visitation so he would blow the trumpet to a slumbering Church, to know what time it is and awake them to the responsibility of taking the Gospel to the ends of the earth - as fast as possible and as far as possible.

Friends, we are living on borrowed time. These are not just the last days, they are the very last seconds of the last days. The bridegroom is at the door. The trumpet is already in the mouth of the angels, about to blow, to herald the return of the Messiah, to take His bride, the Church. The final whistle is about to be blown. The curtain is about to be drawn. All the signs that the Scriptures predicted several years ago are being fulfilled before our very eyes. Alliances are being formed now by the nations for the final battle. The stage is being set for the anti-Christ to show up. The world, as we know it, is racing to an end.

Yet, the Church of the 21st century is exhibiting all the characteristics of the Laodicean Church. We seem to be losing our spiritual fervour; our passion for spiritual things is waning every day and our zeal for finishing the Great Commission is nothing good to write home about. Countless souls are racing to a Christless eternity. About 30% of the world's population are yet without the Good News when Jesus paid the price for all. 39% are still in the valley of decision - having heard the Gospel but have not

committed their souls into the hand of the Man who was crucified for their sake on Calvary. The Church must be awakened to
the time in which we are living - it is now or never! The end of
all things has come. We cannot afford to delay any longer. No
more indifference to the plight of sinners.

Church leaders, we can no longer procrastinate. Jesus warned
us against postponing or thinking there is still time to plunge into
the harvest field. He declared in John's Gospel 4:35 - "Do you
not say, 'There are still four months and then comes the harvest'?
Behold, I say to you, lift up your eyes and look at the fields, for
they are already white for harvest!" (NKJV). We are commanded
to open our eyes now! Look at the field - the Middle East, the
Muslim nations, the whole of Europe and Africa! Lift up your
eyes, India is filled with Hindus. Out of about 7,000 unreached
people groups worldwide, India alone has over 2,000.

Time is short for this world; the earth is in its last seconds and
it would soon be rolled away like a scroll. Sinners are living on
borrowed time and death is fast closing in on multitudes. As I
write this book, many have crossed over to a Christless eternity
without hope in the world to come. Friend, time is short. You are
fast getting old. This is a once-in-a-lifetime opportunity to prove
to Christ how much you love Him. Time is fast closing in on you
to invest your time, talents and treasures in rescuing many out of
hellfire. Time is running out for you to go on that missionary
trip. Time is running out to spend and be spent, to serve Him like
never before.

It is the countdown - to restructure your church or ministry. It
is the countdown - to stop playing church and get on the streets;
plunge into the byways and highways to compel men and
women to come in. We are out of time to hold that crusade, visit
the pris-ons and go to the hospitals. Time is Running Out!

CHAPTER 5

PROSPERITY WITH PURPOSE

"Earn as much as you can, save as much as you can, invest as much as you can, give as much as you can."
– John Wesley

"Nothing is more dangerous than to be blinded by prosperity." – John

Calvin

The saying is true - "When purpose is lost, abuse is inevitable." When we lose the purpose of a thing, abuse automatically kicks in!

One thing is very clear from the Holy Writ - The God of the Bible is a God of purpose and objectivity. Everything He does or creates is with a purpose. When God created man, He had a pur-pose. When He established the Heavens and the earth, He had a clear purpose; for the woman - it was to be a helpmeet to the man. Therefore, any time a woman misses or abuses her purpose, she becomes something else which is not part of God's plan.

We read in Genesis 12:1-3 (NIV):

"The LORD had said to Abram, 'Go from your country, your people and your father's household to the land I will show you. I will make you into a great nation, and I will bless you; I will make your name great, and you will be a blessing. I will bless those who bless you, and whoever curses you I will curse; and all peoples on earth will be blessed through you.'"

Embedded in this call of the Father of Faith is the promise of blessings and greatness. The purpose of the blessing was for him to be a blessing. Abram was, therefore, only meant to be a channel or conduit. God's programme wasn't all about Abram but to include the nations and the families of the earth. Abram was the missionary, called out of his family and comfort zone to be a bless-ing to the Gentile world.

This is always God's modus operandi! God calls a man or wom-an and blesses and empowers him or her to be a blessing to others. The same applies to Israel. They were meant to be a light to the Gentiles, according to Psalm 96:3; they were to declare His glory among the heathen, and His wonders amongst all peoples. When God called Israel out of the committee of nations, it was not be-cause they were better. When He blessed them with the Father's miracles, signs and wonders, it was meant to point others to the God of Israel. Too often, Israel missed their calling. They became introverted as exemplified by the stories of Prophet Jonah and Apostle Peter, who both could not conceive how the God of the Jews could also be the God of the Gentiles. God always prospers or blesses with a purpose. When He gives you children, houses, relationships or money, it is for a purpose. It is never just about you! In 1 Peter 4:10, we are charged to minister whatever gift we have received from the Lord to others as good managers or stew-ards of the manifold Grace of God.

I am a prosperity preacher because prosperity is littered throughout the Old and New Testaments. I believe that Jesus has fully paid for our deliverance, healing, and soundness of mind, among others. His finished work confers on us some covenant rights which include material prosperity.

However, what I consider to be wrong with the brand of our prosperity messages is that it is one-sided - it is too self-centred! It feeds into man's greed. Too often, preachers don't balance their messages with the purpose of the blessing. The brand of prosper-ity messages that many preach, particularly in Africa and North America, stinks. When the missionaries came to Africa, their message was holistic - they brought churches to cater for our spir-its, education to cater for our minds or souls, and hospitals to cater for our bodies. This was one of the major reasons why they reached heathen nations and many people were converted to the Christian Faith.

Many of our messages today are producing greed in the Church. The amount of money and resources locked up in Pentecostal and Charismatic churches - if when released, in my opinion, can ena-ble us to finish the Great Commission in our generation.

Friend, have you asked yourself why God gave you so much money - much more than you and your children will need in their lifetime? Friend, have you considered releasing some of your lands and properties for the propagation of the Gospel? With ten cars parked in your garage, have you considered releasing one for the missionary in the village suffering? Have you considered placing that missionary or man of God on your payroll, with all the mil-lions of dollars, pounds, euros, yen, naira or cedis in your bank account? Jesus, even though He was rich, became poor so that we, through His poverty, may become rich.

God has a plan and a purpose for what He has placed in our hands. Remember, you are saved to save others and also blessed to be a blessing! You are a channel! Can you imagine getting to Heaven and God tells you that several thousands of people would have made Heaven if you had released some of your resources? Remember, you will leave all the money, houses, cars, jewellery etc. here on earth! We all came with nothing and will surely leave with nothing.

There is a burden in the heart of God to take the Gospel to the lost, last and least, but it will take you releasing what is in your hands for this to be accomplished. Will you?

CHAPTER 6

8 MODES OF EVANGELISM

"A church that is not a missionary church is contradicting itself
and quenching the spirit."
– The Lausanne Covenant

"God isn't looking for people of great faith,
but for individuals ready to follow him."
– Hudson Taylor

"Expect great things from God, attempt great things

for God." – William Carey

"Let my heart be broken with the things that break

God's heart." – Bob Pierce

"For though I am free from all men, I have made myself a servant to all, that I might win the more; and to the Jews I became as a Jew, that I might win Jews; to those who are under the law, as under the law, that I might win those who are under the law; to those who are without law, as without law (not being without law toward God, but under law toward Christ), that I might win those who are without law; to the weak I be-came as weak, that I might win the weak. I have become all things to all men that I might by all means save some."

- 1 Corinthians 9:19-22 (NKJV)

One of the most important things anyone serious about soul winning must understand is that there's no single formula or way in leading men and women to Christ. Paul, the great apostle and missionary evangelist, declared that he became all things to all men that he might win some. He employed different methods and strategies to reconcile men to God.

If we are going to be successful in our missionary and evangelistic endeavours in the 21st century, church leaders and believers generally must be aware of the different modes of evangelism and embrace them, so that soul winning can remain a priority.

Important reasons why I am highlighting the various modes of evangelism:

1. To understand the differences between the different modes, and to highlight the fact that individuals can come to salvation through diverse means.

2. To identify what modes would be suitable for different nations and situations. For example, some modes of evangelism will be difficult or almost impossible among some people groups of closed nations.

3. Finally, it is very crucial as Christian leaders and believers to always do a theological reflection of our practices. We must be able to know what we are doing and why. This is generally missing in many streams of Christianity today.

MODES OF EVANGELISM

1. PRESENCE EVANGELISM - This is the first mode of evan-gelism and it is the most basic way to witness in any given society. Usually, the presence of any group of believers in a community or society would always pose peculiar questions, such as - who are these ones, and why are they here?

The emphasis of presence evangelism is not so much our speaking or actions, but rather our presence. The believers' presence should always evoke or raise questions within the hearts of the people in the community. We might speak as occasion demands, but our primary strategy is not speaking. It is critical that ministry leaders and believers in every church family understand this dynamic as our conduct or behaviour will either help or hinder our witness!

This same principle applies to believers operating in all the 7 spheres of society. Two scriptures readily come to mind to help drive home this point. In Matthew 5:13-16, Jesus declared what the vocation of the believer is in the world when he said - "...you are the salt of the earth... and you are the light of the world..." (NIV). Did you notice something similar between these two com-modities? Their impact is felt greatly but never in a vocal manner!

Similarly, Apostle Peter counsels believers on how best to win their unbelieving husbands:

> "Wives, likewise, be submissive to your own husbands, that even if some do not obey the word, they, without a word, may be won by the conduct of their wives, when they observe your chaste conduct accom-panied by fear."
> 1 Peter 3:1-2 (NKJV)

Notice how unbelieving husbands are meant to be won - without a word, but through the conduct or lifestyle of the believing wives.

Our presence as believers in any given society must bring with it a good testimony which will, in turn, attract the unsaved to the light of Christ!

2. PROCLAMATION EVANGELISM - Proclamation is the second mode of evangelism. It means to state or say something in a definite way. It also indicates declaring or making an announcement! The primary focus of proclamation evangelism is to make the Gospel clear. The preacher or gospeller endeavours to explain the Good News. Are you aware that only a few people in the Church of Christ truly proclaim or explain the Gospel? The sim-ple reason is that too many believers themselves don't understand the essence of the Gospel. I have listened to many preachers and believers, and I can state without fear or favour that only a few really explain the Gospel.

Anyone who has listened to Evangelist J. John, the late Rein-hard Bonnke and the late Dr Billy Graham will agree that these men were great proclaimers of the Gospel. In order to proclaim the Gospel clearly, we must study and understand the Scriptures. A wise Christian leader, from time to time, will invite servants of God who are graced in this area to minister in their church.

3. PERSUASION EVANGELISM - This is a contribution of the Arminian school which stresses the importance of individuals responding to the call of God. Since God will never force any-one to be saved, the Arminians reason that the onus now lies on those who share the Gospel, to present it persuasively so that the individual can respond to the message willingly. It is almost like a good salesperson who marshals every argument to convince a person to buy a product or service.

A classic Biblical example of persuasive evangelism was when

Paul the Apostle presented the Gospel to King Agrippa in Acts 26:28. The king's response was -

"…you almost persuade me to become a Christian." (NKJV)

4.   POWER EVANGELISM - Power Evangelism is the spiritual dimension of the Good News, such as healing, miracles, signs and wonders! This has almost been lost in our days! The preaching of the Gospel today can be branded as philosophical speculation or the enticing words of men's wisdom.

If we are being honest with ourselves, most believers have never witnessed genuine healing or miracles, yet we proclaim and advertise that Jesus is alive! Paul encapsulated his ministry when he declared to the Corinthian believers in 1 Corinthians 2:1-5 (NKJV):

"And I, brethren, when I came to you, did not come with excellence of speech or of wisdom declaring to you the testimony of God. For I determined not to know anything among you except Jesus Christ and Him crucified. I was with you in weakness, in fear, and in much trembling. And my speech and my preaching were not with persuasive words of human wisdom, but in demonstration of the Spirit and of power, that your faith should not be in the wisdom of men but in the power of God."

Power Evangelism will work in every society, particularly those that seem "closed" to the Gospel! When Jesus gave us the marching orders of the Great Commission mandate, He promised us supernatural power and manifestations. Mark 16:17-18 (NKJV):

"And these signs will follow those who believe: In My name they will cast out demons; they will speak with new tongues; they will take up serpents; and if they drink anything deadly, it will by no means hurt them; they will lay hands on the sick, and they will recover."

In Acts 9:36-42, Tabitha was raised from the dead. What was the effect? Many received the Gospel! Again, in Acts 13:6-12, as a result of the instant judgement of the magician, Elymas, the Bible declares that the proconsul believed what Paul had preached.

I, wholeheartedly, believe that several thousands, possibly millions, will be swept into the kingdom of God if those of us who preach the Gospel will back it up with supernatural power and manifestations. The big question here is, can we pay the price of supernatural power, since God has never been known to be prodigal with His power?

5. PRAISE AND PRAYER - This mode of evangelism comprises prayer walks and praise marches. This involves turning the focus of the Church outward rather than inward. This mode was popularised in the UK in the 1980s and 1990s by Graham Kendrick with his popular song "Shine Jesus shine, fill this land with the Father's Glory!"

I am convinced that prayer walks and praise marches have a spiritual impact in bringing souls into the Kingdom. Many church leaders have testified of the impact these have made on their tar-get communities after they embarked on them. This is particularly important when you are starting a new work, such as planting a church or embarking on evangelistic or apostolic initiatives.

A Biblical precedence for this mode of evangelism was the cap-ture of Jericho by the Israelites. They marched around the city for 7 days until the city fell! (Joshua 6:1-27)

6. PROGRAMME EVANGELISM - This mode of evangelism is based or anchored on research, analysis and planning.

Programme Evangelism is very much wide-ranging. It could be in a church building, community hall, stadium, hotel, educational institution or a market place.

Churches and Christian Ministries must be very strategic when embarking on programme evangelism, particularly on how best to attract sinners, present the Gospel and bring in the har-vest of souls.

Over the years, the ministry that I lead has used various pro-grammes to reach sinners - these include monthly friends and family services, anniversaries, conventions, and marriage, baby and funeral celebrations, just to mention a few. The important factor here is to use these programmes to bring souls into the Kingdom! The unfortunate reality, however, is that a lot of ministries never utilise their programmes to harvest souls.

The Full Gospel Business Men's Fellowship International is a good example of programme evangelism. Over the decades, they have planned special meetings in posh venues to attract souls into the Kingdom.

7.   **PERSONAL EVANGELISM** - This is the contribution of the evangelical tradition. To be effective as a ministry, church leaders and individual believers must pay serious attention to per-sonal evangelism. This is because, from experience, it is by far the most effective way of bringing sinners to Christ and the Church. Jesus used this mode a lot, as can be seen when He ministered to individuals like Zacchaeus and the Samaritan woman.

The primary reason, in my estimation, for stagnation and decline in church attendance, is mostly traceable to apathy or indifference in personal evangelism. If your ministry has stopped growing, just ask the average person on your pews when last they won a soul or invited someone to fellowship. My guess is as good as yours!

S/N	PROGRAMME	PERCENTAGE
1	Evangelistic Crusade	5%
2	Visitation	1%
3	Special Needs	2%
4	Just Walked into the Church	3%
5	Special Programmes	3%
6	Sunday School	5%
7	Pastor/Minister	6%
8	Friends/Family	75%

A study was done in Pasadena, California, on how people were won to the Lord and joined a local church. The table above high-lights the findings - the various ways and the percentages of how people joined the church:

The verdict! - Personal evangelism is the most strategic key to church growth and populating the Kingdom!

I've been privileged by God to minister in various continents - Europe, Africa, North America, Asia and the Middle East, and have asked believers the same question everywhere I've preached - how did you come to the Faith or join the local church? The response has always been overwhelming - personal evangelism (friends and family)! The key to church growth is never a guest speaker; it is the individual believer! Therefore, church leaders must focus on the people seated on their pews!

8. PROPHETIC EVANGELISM - Prophetic evangelism in-volves employing the revelatory gifts to bring sinners to the Faith. These gifts include Prophecy, Word of Knowledge, Word of Wisdom and the Discerning of Spirits (1 Corinthians 12:4-11).

We all know how much these gifts can and do attract crowds, including sinners. I know of several people who were brought to the Faith because a servant of God with the prophetic gift spoke directly into their lives and situation.

Let's consider what impact the gift of Prophecy could have on the unregenerated:

> "But if all prophesy, and an unbeliever or an uninformed person comes in, he is convinced by all, he is convicted by all. And thus the secrets of his heart are revealed; and so, falling down on his face, he will worship God and report that God is truly among you." - 1 Corinthians 14:24-25 (NKJV)

Can you imagine the impact that Jesus' encounter with the Samaritan woman made in John Chapter 4? Jesus used the revelatory gift to win this woman, who in turn won a whole city - Samaria!

I am eternally grateful for the various men and women whom God has graced with the revelatory gift. One challenge I will love these leaders to consider is - can we use these gifts to lead souls to the Lord, instead of just encouraging and revealing the secrets of men's lives or situations. Prophets must cease demonstrating spiritual showmanship and lead men and women to Christ!

CHAPTER 7

THE SOUL WINNER'S CROWN

"If I thought I could win one more soul to the Lord by walking on my head and playing the Tambourine with my toes, I'd learn how." – William Booth

"God has created me to do him some definite service; He has committed some work to me which he has not committed to another. I have my mission. I may never know it in this life but I shall be told it in the next."
– John Henry Cardinal Newman

"It is the greatest pleasure of living to win souls to Christ." – Dwight L. Moody

God is a master motivator. I have keenly watched institutions, organisations, business enterprises, government corporations and some religious orders, and seen how they encourage, inspire and promise outstanding rewards to their staff when they excel, bring in the highest sales or unparalleled recognition to the organisation.

In the same vein, we read about God promising outstanding rewards to outstanding servants - both in this world and in the world to come. Hebrews 11:6b (NKJV) reads:

"... He is a rewarder of those who diligently seek him."

Matthew chapter 25 (NIV) speaks about God's reward system to his faithful servants:

Verse 23 -

"Well done, good and faithful servant! You have been faithful with a few things; I will put you in charge of many things. Come and share your master's happiness!"

Faithfulness with what has been committed into our trust on earth is rewarded with rulership in the Kingdom to come. Conversely, the unfaithful servant will be reprimanded or rebuked for being lazy and not putting to use what had been committed into his trust.

Verses 26-30 -

"You wicked, lazy servant! So you knew that I harvest where I have not sown and gather where I have not scattered seed? Well then, you should have put my money on deposit with the bankers, so that when I returned I would have received it back with interest. So take the bag of gold from him and give it to the one who has ten bags. For whoever has will be given more, and they will have an abundance. Whoever does not have, even what they have will be taken from them. And throw that worthless servant outside, into the darkness, where there will be weeping and gnashing of teeth."

From this passage, we can conclude that rewards for serving God or Christ faithfully in this present age will consist of positions of authority and responsibility in the administration of Christ's Kingdom in the coming age. For soul winners, those who will lead sinners away from the path of destruction and death, those who are not ashamed to share the glorious Gospel of Christ from

Jerusalem to the uttermost parts of the earth, God has promised them greater rewards in the age to come.

One of such rewards is the Crown of Rejoicing. The Crown of Rejoicing is also known as the "Crown of Exaltation" or the "Crown of Auxiliary".

To the Thessalonian believers who had been converted to the ministry of Apostle Paul, he remarked -

"For what is our hope, our joy, or the crown in which we will glory in the presence of our Lord Jesus when he comes? Is it not you? Indeed, you are our glory and joy."
- 1 Thessalonians 2:19-20 (NIV)

The Thessalonian Christians who had been converted and disci-pled through the ministry of Paul the Apostle are his Joy, Hope, and Crown of Rejoicing in the presence of the Lord at His coming.

Again, in Philippians 4:1 (NKJV) -

"Therefore, my beloved and longed-for brethren, my joy and crown, so stand fast in the Lord, beloved."

Notice how Paul addressed his spiritual children in the city of Philippi. He refers to them as his joy and crown. They were ad-monished to stand strong in the Lord. Glory! Glory! Glory! Glory!

I feel excited and joyful as I call to mind times and places where I have laboured to bring people to the Lord. I call to mind our evangelistic outreach to Ibeju village on the outskirts of Lagos around the mid-1980s, I call to mind several souls that were saved from the medium and maximum prisons in Kirikiri, Lagos be-tween 1985 and 1988. I recall various outreach programmes in the Federal Capital Territory of Nigeria between 1988 and 1989

- outreaches to Abaji, Robochi, Gwagwalada, Wuse and Gariki. I call to mind many that were snatched at the point of death at the Lagos University Hospital wards in the late 1980s.

I remember our labour for almost 30 years in Britain, Wales, Scotland, the Caribbean, Burkina Faso, Benin Republic and India! I call to mind Sylvester - a French brother led to the Lord on the streets of Camberwell, London, who transited to glory about 15 years ago. I am filled with joy as I call to mind several souls that have been led to the Savior as I have journeyed across over 25 states in America, planted works in Canada, Liberia, Benin Republic, Ghana and Congo. I call to mind a gentleman who was led to the Lord mid-air on my way to minister in South Africa. I call to mind ex-Muslims who were led to the Lord in Turkey and many more who found the Saviour through my ministry in the United Arab Emirates. I feel super-excited about the thought of getting crowns at His appearing. At the same time, I feel a heavy burden to depopulate hell and awake the sleeping giants to our responsibility towards finishing the Great Commission in our generation.

I have a burning vision and passion to have converts from my ministry efforts - either directly or indirectly, who will be in Heav-en from every nation of the earth. I have an unquenchable desire to see saints from every single nation coming to hug me and say thank you - I am in Heaven because you prayed, gave and came. I want to take as many people to Heaven as possible. This is why I have set, as my primary assignment, to be a catalyst in reach-ing the unreached with the Gospel and mobilising the Church to rise to our most important assignment - Souls! Souls! Souls! And Souls!

In the book of Daniel 12:3 (NKJV), we read:

"Those who are wise shall shine like the brightness of the firmament, and those who turn many to righteousness like the stars forever and ever."

Today, many try to be stars in the world of entertainment only to find their stardom temporary. God tells us how we can be "eternal stars" by being wise and leading many to God's righteousness. If we can share our Lord and Saviour, Jesus Christ, with others, then we can be true stars - radiantly beautiful in God's sight.

Three things you must begin to do immediately to receive a soul winner's crown. You must:

1. Go personally - go everywhere with the Gospel
2. Give sacrificially - towards all soul-winning endeavours
3. Pray globally - that those who do not know Him will find Him

and that the scales of unbelief will be removed from their eyes.

It is time to arise! It's time to wake up! It's time to win Souls.

No delays! No apathy! No excuses!

CHAPTER 8

WHY WE NEED TO TRAIN AND DISCIPLE

"The one indispensable requirement for producing
godly, mature Christians is godly, mature Christians."
- Kevin DeYoung

"If you really want to experience God, go and make
disciples." - Francis Chan

"God has entrusted us with his most precious treasure - People. He
asks us to Shepherd and mould them into Strong disciples, with brave
faith and good character." - John Ortberg

Let us consider the following statistics of the unreached people
groups, according to the Joshua Project:

- The World's population stands at about 7.67 billion.
- The total number of people groups is 17,423.
- The unreached people groups are 7,410.

The total population among the unreached people groups is 3.19
billion, constituting about 41.6% of the world's population. These
people mostly don't have any Christian presence - no living

church, no minister of the Gospel, have never read the Living Word of God and are in total darkness, without God and hope in this world. Most of these unreached people groups are geographically located in what is referred to as "the 10/40 window". This comprises the Eastern hemisphere as well as the European and African parts of the Western hemisphere that are located between 10 and 40 degrees, north of the Equator.

The global statistics of Christians reveal that the percentage of genuine Christians today is between 10% and 11% of the world's population.

Why am I giving these statistics, you may ask? It is to answer a very strategic question - how is the Church going to take the Gospel to these people who have never heard the Good News? How are we going to make sure that no one ends up in hell due to our indifference, negligence and lukewarmness?

There are two options open to us:

1. To depend mostly on the Doma gifts or the Ephesians chap-ter 4 equipping ministries of Apostles, Prophets, Evangelists, Pastors and Teachers, as we have been doing for several dec-ades. To execute this mammoth challenge, we have adopted a 'superstar' model whereby our church leaders or the few "professionals" take the bulk of the burden for witnessing and missionary endeavours, while the majority of believers, simply assume the roles of onlookers, spectators and benchwarm-ers, who are entertained weekly in glass-stained cathedrals. I must concede that there's a place, biblically, for evangelistic and missionary endeavours such as stadium crusades or mass meetings led by evangelists and other ministers of the Gos-pel. We can all testify, for example, of the impact and fruits that have stemmed from meetings held around the world by

faithful servants of God, such as the late Dr Billy Graham and Reinhard Bonnke. Also, we can and we have used the model whereby pastors or elders have been used as the arrowhead in our evangelistic enterprises. This happens when pastors and elders use their local fellowships as a platform for soul winning. This is particularly effective if we are involved in massive church planting campaigns. I am one of those who have bought into the theory propounded by the late foremost missiologist of the 20th Century, Peter Wagner, who said: "church planting is the most effective evangelistic method un-der heaven". Classical examples in modern times include the global exploits of the Redeemed Christian Church of God, led by Pastor E. A. Adeboye, or the Lighthouse Church, led by Bishop Dag Heward-Mills.

2. The second option is what I believe in and I am proposing if we are going to finish the Great Commission in our generation. It is to disciple and train the frontline soldiers - the Christian masses who fill churches weekly, simply to come and be entertained. These masses constitute at least 95% of the Church's workforce. The strategy and emphasis must be to disciple, train and release them. We must go beyond be-ing satisfied with asking people to show a raise of the hands, join our churches, and then keep them perpetually in the four corners of our walls, only to boost our ego of "pastoring a large congregation!" Most often than not, these people are not taken through proper rigorous discipleship programmes as it used to be several decades ago. This is why, I believe, the aver-age member of our churches cannot point to a single person they have won or discipled for the Lord in the last 1 year, and sometimes even 10 years. There are many elders sitting on our

boards and committees who do not even know how to

present the Gospel or disciple new converts.

Our emphasis must change to winning, rooting, discipling, empowering and releasing the masses into the world—into Jerusalem, Judea, Samaria and to the utmost parts of the world. We must begin to identify those in the 7 spheres of society and train, affirm and release them to take the light of the Gospel into the areas of government and politics, economy and distribution, education, family, media, religion, and entertainment - sports, fashion, music, art and so on! We must be the light where there's darkness - OUTSIDE the walls of our churches!

This was the model adopted by Jesus to reach His world. He chose disciples and spent two-thirds of His time with them - modelling, mentoring and monitoring them. He poured Himself into these 12 and then released them into the world - these were men who were described by the society as unlearned, yet succeed-ed in turning the world upside down for Jesus. We need to follow this pattern.

The Early Church also followed this model. They raised disciples after their kind, as exemplified by the ministry of Paul, who raised Timothy and Titus, and many others. John, the revelator, raised many, among whom was the 2nd Century Bishop of Smyrna - Polycarp. This is the model I am endeavouring to practice as our time is very short. It is a 2-pronged strategy:

• First, I want to personally reach out to sinners wherever I am privileged by God to meet them - on the road, in the market, on the train, bus, plane, church setting or the mountains and jungles in India.

• Secondly, and possibly more strategically, is to disciple, train, and pour my life into people through short conferences, semi-nars, workers training programmes, leadership empowerment meetings, university and student training, and church plant-ing training, etc. The purpose is to inspire, educate, equip and release as many into the harvest field, who would also repli-cate same.

This was what Paul meant when he wrote to his protégé, Timothy, in 2 Timothy 2:2 (NIV) - "And the things you have heard me say in the presence of many witnesses entrust to reliable people who will also be qualified to teach others." This is the Four Genera-tion Discipleship Programme which is the key to completing the Great Commission:

- Paul – 1st generation
- Timothy – 2nd generation
- Reliable/Faithful Men – 3rd generation
- Others – 4th generation

Let me conclude by raising these two challenges:

First, to pastors and ministry leaders - let our focus in ministry be to disciple, train and release the saints into ministry. You must stop spoon-feeding and entertaining the people. You must intro-duce new structures and programmes that will service this model. We might have to change our preaching style and ministry focus.

Secondly, I want to challenge all Believers (most of the peo-ple reading this book will fall into this category). You must stop going to church to be entertained. You must grow up and take responsibility for your Christian walk. Start studying your Bible more than ever. Get to know Jesus by yourself. Invest in Christian classics (books); readers are leaders! Then please, take personal responsibility for soul winning. Set soul-winning targets for yourself. Get up and go! Go to the highways and byways and share Jesus. Take the Gospel into politics, business, media, sports and education! Stop hiding Jesus in your house! Stop keeping Him in your handbag! Muslims are not ashamed to pray anywhere - including in their businesses. You are the key to finishing the Great Commission. Leave a legacy and attempt great things for God!

CHAPTER 9

WHY EVERY LEADER OUGHT TO BE
A SOUL WINNER

"A good leader leads the people from above them. A great leader leads the people from within them." - M. D. Arnold

"Don't follow the crowd, let the crowd follow you."
- Margaret Thatcher

"The task of the leader is to get their people from where they are to where they have not been." - Henry Kissinger

"Let no man despise thy youth; but be thou an example of the believers, in word, in conversation, in charity, in spirit, in faith, in purity."
– 1 Timothy 4: 12 (KJV).

I decided to add this chapter in because leadership is so crucial to any venture. The success or failure of anything often depends on the quality of its leadership. I am a firm believer of the fact that all ministry leaders are first and foremost called to soul winning, after which their giftings, anointing or grace for other unique areas of ministry follow.

Here are a few reasons why I think every spiritual leader ought to be Soul Winner:

1. Every spiritual leader is called to do the work of an evangelist.

"But watch thou in all things, endure afflictions, do the work of an evangelist, make full proof of thy ministry." - 2 Timothy 4:5 (KJV)

In the above passage, we see the Apostle Paul giving a charge to the pastor or bishop of the church in Ephesus to do the work of an evangelist! Even though Timothy, a spiritual leader, wasn't an evangelist by calling, he was expected to do the work of an evangelist. Therefore, by assumption, all church leaders, no matter their title or call, should also do the work of an evangelist. This is so because soul winning is the primary assignment of the Church.

2. Jesus was a soul winner! No doubt, Jesus is our perfect example and leader. No servant can be greater than his master. If there was an important reason why church leaders must be soul winners, it is because Jesus was a soul winner par excellence! He not only spoke to crowds but also converted individuals. Two ex-amples that come to mind are the Samaritan woman and the con-version of Zacchaeus.

3. A Good Shepherd, according to the parable of Jesus, would leave the ninety-nine sheep that are saved and go after the lost sheep, until it is found (Luke 15:4-7). Today, the opposite seems to be taking place.

4. Missions vs Maintenance - once a pastor or a ministry leader is not, or ceases to be missions-minded - ever reaching out for souls, he sets into the maintenance mode. Maintenance-minded leaders or believers would always give or look for all conceivable reasons under the sun to make the ministry look "better" or to solve a problem, without necessarily adding new souls to the fold.

5. The Danger of Persecution - Quite often, when we refuse to win souls or extend the frontiers of the Church, God allows persecution or challenges to get us doing the job. In other words, he forces us into soul winning. I have always argued that if the Church of Christ refuses to willingly embrace Acts 1:8, Acts 8:1 will, definitely, be our experience! Jonah encountered serious challenges as a leader because he refused to carry out Heaven's bidding.

6. Access To Financial and Divine Resources - There's always a correlation between soul winning and financial empowerment. Churches, ministries and leaders who are soul winners never get stranded financially. What was Jesus' answer to the financial embarrassment of paying taxes? - go and catch a fish, once you open its mouth, that fish will produce the money (Matthew 17:27)!
Most of our financial needs in the Church today are in the mouth of the fish - souls that are yet to be harvested. Remember, we are called to be Fishers of Men! Jesus' primary assignment for His leaders was for them to be soul winners.

"Follow me... and I will make you Fishers of Men [or soul

winners]." – Matthew 4:19

7. The command of the Great Commission was given to every believer or Christian and we must never forget that church leaders are first and foremost Christians before leaders or pastors (Matthew 28:18-20 & Mark 16:15-20).

8. Pastors and church leaders must always be mindful that soul winning is not optional for them.

> "For necessity is laid upon me; yea, woe is unto me, if I preach not the gospel!"
> – 1 Corinthians 9:16 (KJV)

9. Because the success of soul-winning endeavours is often linked to the efforts, vision and example of leaders. The saying is very true - "like father, like son!" Like children, church members, more often than not, always follow the example of their pastors and leaders. Therefore, if pastors and leaders don't regularly win souls, the Church is on its way to extinction!

10. The reward of the soul winner's crown which is also called the Crown of Rejoicing.

> "For what is our hope, or joy, or crown of rejoicing? Are not even ye in the presence of our Lord Jesus Christ at his coming?" – 1 Thessalonians 2:19 (KJV)

CHAPTER 10

HOW TO TURN YOUR CHURCH INTO
A SOUL-WINNING MOVEMENT

"Go for souls. Go straight for souls, and go for

the worst." – William Booth

"I just want to lobby for God."
– Billy Graham

"My people are destroyed for lack of knowledge."
– Hosea 4:6 (KJV)

A reoccurring question that I am asked whenever I travel around the world is – "how can I turn things around in my church?" or "how can we become passionate about soul winning?"

A church leader once approached me and remarked - "I know that we should be winning souls and reaching out to our com-munity but it is just not happening, and I'm really frustrated." One thing I can assure you of is that this pastor is not alone - many church leaders are experiencing same. It is a known fact that church stagnation is one of the key reasons why many pastors are leaving the ministry and it is a major headache for others. So, what can we do if the above picture paints our present situation as a ministry or church and how can we turn things around?

I do not claim to be a church growth or evangelism expert, but I would like to offer my humble advice. These are my 'five loaves and two fishes:

1. **Have a Clear & Proactive Evangelism Vision** - The most important factor or ingredient in turning a ministry into an evangelistic or soul-winning movement is vision.

   "Where there is no Vision, the people perish."

   - Proverbs 29:18 (KJV).

   Where there is no clear vision, the people run wild - they cast off restraint!

   Today, many churches and ministries are running wild because there is no clear vision for soul winning or the missionary enterprise. I have read so many vision statements of several ministries and have found some declare that they are called by God to raise leaders in the society, whereas others profess that their mandate is to make members prosperous or the high-flyers in their communities. While all these may be valid, I am of the opinion that converting the souls of men and making them candidates of Heaven supersedes every other goal.

   The first and most important assignment of any leader or Christian ministry is to take people to Heaven. This must be stated clearly and must be our global vision. It should, therefore, drive everything we do. We must express this important vision in a variety of ways; through our songs, confessions on our walls, banners, in our quotes, as anthems and so on! We need to be very creative in doing this.

   Leaders must challenge their followers regularly with important quotes like:

"Any church that is not seriously involved in helping
fulfil the great commission has forfeited its biblical
right to exist." - Oswald J. Smith

"Soul-winning is the chief business of the Christian minister; It should
be the main pursuit of every true believer." - Charles Spurgeon

"The only alternative to soul winning is disobedience to Christ." -
Curtis Hutson

The importance of a clear vision is that it is what rallies the
community to a common cause! Pastor, when people come to
your ministry, can they see, smell, hear and feel the passion
for souls? If not, you might need to re-examine your vision.

2. **Structure** - The second important key or ingredient towards
   turning any ministry into a soul-winning movement is structure. Our structure would either help or hinder church growth
   and the evangelistic enterprise. Businesses require structure
   to grow and be profitable, otherwise, you would have people
   running in all sorts of direction. The same applies to
   Christian organisations. A very important question that I
   would like to raise is - how many of our present structures
   aid or contribute to soul winning? It is safe to say that many
   of our ministries are structured for maintenance and not
   missions. Our struc-tures are often created to maintain the
   status quo and not for outreach.

   In order to turn our ministries into evangelistic and mis-

   sionary movements, we must re-evaluate our structures. You

might have to bring down some structures and raise others.

3. **Personnel** - We are all conversant with the idiomatic expression "a square peg in a round hole or a round peg in a square hole". It speaks of a misfit, especially a person unsuited for a position or activity. Nothing is more frustrating in an evangelistic or church enterprise than having the wrong person in a strategic position. For example, a ministry that wants to be on the cutting edge of the evangelistic and missionary enterprise cannot fill its strategic positions with administrators or managers, even though they may be important personnel.

As a church planter, I have come to the unreserved conclusion that a pastor (church planter) is the most important person in the success of a new church. Sadly enough, there are some church leaders who will not push for evangelism or church growth; they're simply not motivated. If we are going to reach new heights in soul winning, we must have personnel whose remit is not only in the Church but in society. They must have a burden for soul winning; people who will do an-ything and give up everything to make sure they reach the lost at all cost. Some of these persons include pastors, elders, bishops, deacons, trustees, children and youth pastors, school principals, directors and administrators.

It is important for every pioneer and ministry leader to pon-der over these questions:

- Who are your strategic personnel?
- Do they carry the burden for soul-winning or do they need to be pushed?

4. **Messages** - The saying is true - "You are what you eat." One of the key things medical personnel are having to challenge

people to do is to make lifestyle changes. If we are going to live a healthy life, one of the key areas of change is what we eat. As it is in the natural, so it is in the spiritual.

When pastors complain to me about their members being lukewarm and indifferent towards the most important work of the Church – soul winning, one of the first things I want to find out from them is what have you been feeding them with? What has been the central thrust of your messages? You cannot be preaching on prosperity, deliverance, breakthrough and the like, and expect to raise a congregation with missions and evangelism as their heartbeat.

I have come to discover that church leaders are one of the greatest hindrances to an evangelistic movement in their min-istries. I guarantee you - if you will radically change your menu to a Christ-honouring, soul-winning diet, you will be amazed how this will reflect on the drive of your church members.

CHAPTER 11

GOD'S DREAM TEAM

"I want the whole Christ for my Saviour, the whole Bible for my Book,
the whole Church for my Fellowship, and the whole World for my
Mission Field." - John Wesley

"The greatest form of praise is the sound of consecrated feet
seeking out the lost and helpless."
- Billy Graham

"The church which is not a missionary church will be a missing church
when Jesus comes." – F. B. Meyer

God has a Dream Team which most people are unaware of. This dream team was conceived in the heart of God before the foundations of the world. John, the revelator, on the island of Patmos, was shown a glimpse of this dream team and he described it in the apocalypses.

Notice who this team consists of:

"After these things I looked, and behold, a great multitude which no one could number, of all nations, tribes, peoples, and tongues, standing before the throne and before the Lamb, clothed with white robes, with palm branches in their hands, and crying out with a loud voice, saying, "Salvation belongs to our God who sits on the throne, and to the Lamb!" All the angels stood around the throne and the elders and the four living creatures, and fell on their faces before the throne and worshiped God, saying: "Amen! Blessing and glory and wisdom, Thanksgiving and honor and power and might, Be to our God forever and ever. Amen."

Then one of the elders answered, saying to me, "Who are these arrayed in white robes, and where did they come from?" And I said to him, "Sir, you know." So he said to me, "These are the ones who come out of the great tribulation, and washed their robes and made them white in the blood of the Lamb.

Therefore they are before the throne of God, and serve Him day and night in His temple. And He who sits on the throne will dwell among them. They shall neither hunger anymore nor thirst anymore; the sun shall not strike them, nor any heat; for the Lamb who is in the midst of the throne will shepherd them and lead them to living fountains of waters. And God will wipe away every tear from their eyes."

- Revelation 7:9-17 (NKJV)

This team has been gathering for the past 2,000 years! Notice the composition - they are a great multitude which no one can number. They are from every nation, tribe, people and tongue. Therefore, no single nation, tribe, people or tongue on earth is missing; everyone is represented. They were singing before the Throne of God and before the Lamb. They were worshipping!

It is worthy of note that any time the New Testament script mentions the word 'nation', it isn't referring to geographical entities like Great Britain, France, Ghana, Jamaica, Australia or Namibia. It is referring to people groups. It is for the same reason when Christ gave the Church the Great Commission mandate, His instruction was - "Go therefore and make disciples of all nations, baptizing them in the name of the Father, and of the son, and of the Holy Spirit" - Matthew 28:19 (NKJV). The word 'nation' in the New Testament lexicon is 'ethnos', which refers to peo-ple or ethnic groups, of which we have about 17,000 throughout the world.

The intriguing thing about this team is that for the past 2,000 years, they have been gathering as an orchestra, but they cannot sing at the moment for the Lamb, as shown to John, the revelator. The simple reason is that God's dream team is incomplete because Jesus died for the whole world - He paid the price for all mankind to be reconciled back to their maker, and every people group on earth must be represented at this final gathering. This group can't sing yet as they're waiting patiently for representatives from every people group or ethnos.

Did you know?:

- There are still about 19 'ethnos' out of a total of 111 in Ghana yet to be represented.

- Nigeria, my place of birth, is missing 79 people groups out of a total of 544, with a total population of about 53 million - the largest of these groups are the Hausa and Fulani with a combined population of around 40 million.

- Liberia has 5 unreached people groups out of a total of 39, representing a little over half a million people.

- With a total of 509 people groups, there are 502 unreached people groups in Pakistan, according to the Joshua Project.

- Out of a total of 285 people groups in Nepal, 275 representing 96.5% of their population is unreached, which is almost 26 million people.

- Saudi Arabia has a total of 44 people groups. 28 of them are yet to be reached. That is over 30 million of their total population of about 34 million.

- India, by far has the largest population of the unreached people groups in the world. Out of 2,718 people groups, 2,445 are unreached in India. The population of the unreached in India is a little over 1.3 billion people.

By unreached people groups, we mean those who have never heard the Gospel, have no access to a Bible, a missionary, fellow-ship, and, therefore, totally hopeless as far as eternity is concerned.

This is the purpose of this message - to sensitize you about God's incomplete dream team; to let you know that Christ is eagerly waiting for the reward of His sacrifice among every nation, tribe and tongue.

This is why I was born. This is the reason for which I was set apart from my mother's womb - to raise my voice like a trumpet and alert my brethren who are having parties every single Sunday; some with five, ten, twenty, or even fifty thousand members, who are mostly recycled Christians, while sadly ignoring the people who need the Gospel the most.

I have often reiterated that there are 3 important things that every one of us can and should do to help speed up the assembling of God's dream team:

1. Go personally - Decide to visit countries that are without the Gospel and invest your life there.

2. Pray globally - Begin to pray specifically for unreached people groups. Pastors, bear these people groups up in prayer on your altars, rather than self-centred, God-dishonoring prayers every week.

3. Give sacrificially - Many of you business persons and Kingdom financiers must begin to sow where it is needed the most. Support missionaries and ministries who carry a genuine vi-sion for the unreached people. This is your greatest invest-ment. Will you respond?

CHAPTER 12

WHAT IS THE GOSPEL MESSAGE?

"God has given Believers the responsibility of spreading the Gospel to all the world, and we need to use all at our disposal to accomplish this task."

- Theodore H. Epp

"If your souls were not immortal and you in danger of losing them, I would not thus speak unto you; but the love of your souls constrains me to speak: methinks this would constrain me to speak unto you forever."

- George Whitefield

I have listened to several Christians, both leaders and the average believer, share their faith. While some can be applauded for being excellent communicators, theologically-sound and easy to under-stand, I have, however, found the majority preaching every other message except the Gospel of Christ.

A lot of believers think that by inviting sinners to their fellow-ship, they have preached the Gospel. Also, some have focused their attention on the subject of hellfire. While the Gospel has implications and all unbelievers will end up in hell, only a few of us are sharing the Gospel from a Biblical perspective. I have found it necessary to give a simple, yet Biblical synopsis of the Gospel message. May I state that you can always begin the Gospel message from different standpoints. I must also concede that there are many who have shared and preached a message that one could consider very far from the Gospel, yet it pleased the Lord to use it to draw sinners to Himself, extend the borders of His Kingdom and glorify His Name.

For effective witnessing or Gospel presentation, I always suggest the 'ROMANS ROAD' –

1. **The Predicament** – This speaks of man's problem. The Bible paints the picture of man being a sinner and, therefore, lost. "For all have sinned and come short of the glory of God" - Romans 3:23 (KJV). We are sinners not because of the sins we have committed but because we were born sinners. We inherited sin from the first man, Adam. This is why David declared –

   "I was sharpened in iniquity and in sin did my mother conceive me." - Psalm 51:5 (KJV)

   As lost sinners, there is absolutely nothing we can do to rem-edy our situation.

2. **The Penalty** – Sin must be punished. The Bible declares in Romans 6:23 –

   "…the wages of sin is death…" (KJV).

   Sin pays wages and the wages is death.

   There are three types of deaths the Bible speaks of:

a. **Spiritual death:** This is a separation between God and man. Until Adam ate the forbidden fruit and sinned, he had perfect communion with God. However, immediately he sinned, he was cut off from the life of God and communion with God. Anyone outside of Christ today is spiritually dead.

b. **Physical death:** After Adam sinned, he didn't die natu-rally immediately, even though he was cut off from God spiritually. However, after some time, he died physically. This is the lot of all humans except the generation that experiences the rapture. One thing I also noticed after Adam sinned is the fact that the lifespan of humans began to decrease steadily. Would you believe that some of our ancestors in the book of Genesis lived for 900, 800, 700, 600 years? It is almost inconceivable for our minds today.

c. **Eternal death:** Eternal death is also referred to as the second death. "And whosoever was not found written in the book of life was cast into the lake of fire" - Revelation 20:15 (KJV) – this is the second death. Eternal death speaks of eternal damnation. Anyone who rejects Christ and His Gospel is bound to suffer eternal death or dam-nation.

3. **The Provision:** God has made provision for man's predica-ment – sin. This provision is clearly expressed in several Bib-lical passages such as John 3:16 (KJV) –

"For God so loved the world, that He gave His only begotten Son, that whosoever believeth in Him should not perish but have everlasting life."

Again,

"But God commandeth His love toward us, in that, while we were yet sinners, Christ died for us."
- Romans 5:8 (KJV)

a. **Grace and not works!** God's way of accessing His provision is by Grace (God's Riches At Christ's Expense). Grace speaks of God's unmerited favour. Many people have never experienced God's salvation because they try to achieve it through their own means or works. This is called religion. Religion always acts as a stumbling block against the free workings of God's Grace. Ephesians 2:8-9 (NKJV),

"For by grace you have been saved through faith, and that not of yourselves; it is the gift of God, not of works, lest anyone should boast."

b. **Jesus is the only way or accepted sacrifice.** It is very im-portant in our Gospel presentation to state categorically that Jesus is not one of the ways, but the only way to God. New age and other forms of religious dogma teach that there are several ways that lead to the same God. Nothing can be farther from the truth.

"Neither is there salvation in any other: for there is none other name given among men, whereby we must be saved."
- Acts 4:12 (KJV).

Also, read Romans 5:12-15.

c. **Commitment**: I always insist that whatever we do in our Gospel presentation, we must always endeavour to get the sinner to the point of making a commitment. The expe-rienced salesman understands that he is only after one thing – to make a sale. He is not just out to introduce the product, but to persuade the hearer to become a buyer. It is the same for all those who share the Gospel. We must warn against postponing the Day of Salvation, as no one has been promised tomorrow.

"Now is the accepted time; behold, now is the Day of

Salvation." -2 Corinthians 6:2 (NKJV)

Romans 10:9-10 clarifies the way of salvation -

"That if you confess with your mouth the Lord Jesus and believe in your heart that God has raised Him from the dead, you will be saved. For with the heart one believes unto righteousness, and with the mouth confession is made unto salvation."(NKJV)

CHAPTER 13

7 PRAYER KEYS FOR EFFECTIVE EVANGELISM

"We can reach our world, if we will. The
greatest lack today is not people or funds.
The greatest need is prayer." – Wesley
Duewel

"If you take missions out of the Bible,
you won't have anything left but the
covers." – Nina Gunter

"Prayer is the mighty engine that is to move the missionary
work." – A. B. Simpson

Undoubtedly, prayer is the most strategic, yet, most underutilised and most neglected resource in world evangelism. If we are going to take the mandate of the Great Commission seriously, then we must focus more of our energies on this important key.

As Jesus travelled around villages, towns and cities preaching the Gospel of the Kingdom, He saw the crowds and had compas-sion on them because they were harassed and helpless, like sheep without a shepherd. What was Jesus' recommendation? A Com-mittee meeting? An Elders or deacons meeting? Absolutely not!

He recommended a Prayer meeting:

"Then he said to his disciples, 'The harvest is plentiful but the workers are few. Ask the Lord of the harvest, therefore, to send out workers into his harvest field."
– Matthew 9:37-38 (NIV)

Again, in the Messianic Psalm 2, verse 8 declares:

"Ask of Me, and I will give You The nations for Your inheritance,

And the ends of the earth for Your possession." (NKJV)

Let us consider the seven (7) prayer keys for effective evangelism:

1. Pray committedly:

"One day Peter and John were going up to the temple at the time of prayer – at three in the afternoon."
– Acts 3:1 (NIV)

Did you notice that Peter and John had hours of prayer? Throughout the Book of Acts, you will notice that there were "hours of prayer". In the Old Testament, there were prayer watches throughout the day, thus demonstrating a high level of commitment. Today, our prayers seem to be sporadic. We must understand that we cannot win the world, particularly the unreached people groups without strategic and commit-ted prayers. Do you have an hour of prayer? What about your ministry, do they have hours set aside to pray for the salvation of souls? This might be the reason why we have been unable to complete the Great Commission in the last two thousand years.

2. **Pray fervently:** Prayers that change history are always short but fervent.

"The effectual fervent prayer of a righteous man availeth much." – James 5:16 (KJV)

Elijah is a classic example of a righteous man who prayed fervently. He prayed and a whole nation turned to God. The same can be said of John Knox who prayed, "Give me Scotland or I die."

3. **Pray specifically:** Why will a God who is Omniscient still ask us to make requests? It is because He wants us to be specific in our prayers. When most people pray, they do so amiss. In Matthew 16:19 (NIV), Jesus declares –

"Whatever you bind on earth will be bound in heaven, and whatever you loose on earth will be loosed in heaven."

John Praying Hyde prayed – "Give me eight souls a day or I die". How about you pray for a soul a week?

4. **Pray unitedly:** Individual prayers are great but united prayers are more potent, particularly when we begin to pray about what is nearest and dearest to God's heart. In Acts chapter 4, the Church experienced its first persecution. What did they do? After the threats against the Early Church, they went back to their own company –

"When they heard this, they raised their voices together in prayer
to God."
– Acts 4:24 (NIV).

There is multiplied power and grace when we pray with others.
One shall chase a thousand and two shall chase ten thousand
(Deuteronomy 32:30). Jesus declared that:

"My House shall be called a House of

Prayer." – Matthew 21:13 (KJV)

and not a House of Preaching. Prophet Isaiah puts it more suc-
cinctly –

"Even them I will bring to My holy mountain and make them joyful
in My house of prayer. Their burnt offerings and their sacrifices **will**
be accepted on My Altar, for My House shall be called a house of
prayer for all nations."
– Isaiah 56:7 (NKJV).

Did you notice that God's House is meant to be a House of
Prayer for all nations and not just for our personal needs?

5. **Pray persistently:** To be effective in our soul-winning endeavours, we must be persistent in our prayers. One of the
   key principles that the Lord taught on prayer is persistence.
   We have to keep Knocking, Asking and Seeking:

   "So I say to you: Ask and it will be given to you; seek and you
   will find knock and the door will be opened to you."
   - Luke 11:9 (NIV).

Whenever we are praying for the unsaved and the unreached people groups, it might sometimes take weeks, months, years or even our lifetime before our prayers are answered. I once heard a story of a great servant of God who went everywhere preaching the Gospel with several thousands committing their lives to Christ, yet his son was very far from the Lord. This man prayed for weeks, months and years. One year passed on to another without this young man getting saved, yet his father never gave up praying for his salvation. Finally, his father passed unto glory without seeing his son commit his heart to the Lord.

It was at the funeral of his dad when the call was made that this young man committed his heart to the Lord. I am certain it was the persistent prayers of his father that finally yielded results at the due season. This is a great lesson for all those who want to see the unsaved come unto the Kingdom of God.

6. **Pray boldly:** Hebrews 4:16 enjoins us to come boldly to the Throne of God.

    "Let us therefore come boldly unto the throne of grace, that we may obtain mercy, and find grace to help in time of need." (KJV)

    A believer's boldness in prayer must be based on two things:

    a. **The name of Jesus** – We are guaranteed that whatsoever we ask in His name, the Father will do it.

    b. **Praying according to the Will of God** –

        "This is the confidence we have in approaching God: that if we ask anything according to His will, He hears

us." - 1 John 5:14 (NIV)

Nothing is dearer to God's heart, more than praying for the salvation of sinners.

7. **Pray expectantly:** When we pray, we must pray with faith or a confident assurance.

> "This is the confidence we have in approaching God, that if we ask anything according to His will, He hears us. And if we know that He hears us whatever we ask – we know that we have what we asked of Him."
> –1 John 5: 14-15 (NIV)

It is very possible to pray yet without an expectation. In Acts 12, the Church was praying for the release of Peter, yet when the answer came, they were not expecting it. Do you sometimes pray, yet without expecting the answers? It seems this is the practice of many. When we pray, we must pray with great anticipation and expectation from a Great God.

CHAPTER 14

WHERE IS YOUR TREASURE?

"When God blesses you financially, don't raise your standard of living. Raise your standard of giving." - Mark Batterson

"Make all you can, save all you can, give all you can." - John Wesley

"The only thing we can keep are the things we freely give to God…" - C. S. Lewis

"After giving something to God, you are no longer accountable for it. Your blessing is based on your giving, not on what others do with the gift." - Ed Cole

"The way you store up treasure in Heaven is by investing in getting people there." - Rick Warren

"Do not store up for yourselves treasures on earth, where moths and vermin destroy, and where thieves break in and steal. But store up for yourselves treasures in heaven, where moths and vermin do not destroy, and where thieves do not break in and steal. For where your treasure is, there your heart will be also." – Matthew 6:19-21 (NIV)

In this passage, Jesus gives a clear direction regarding where a believer is to store their treasures – Heaven. Never on Earth! This is because earthly treasures are temporal. No matter how valuable they are - gold, silver, diamonds, money, expensive cars and hous-es, all these will pass away with the present world! On the other hand, heavenly treasures are eternal - they will last throughout eternity.

Let me ask you a serious question - if I were to ask you to list the three most important things in your life, what will they be? Again, if your house were to be on fire, what items would you rescue before leaving - money, gold, silver, car, children, wife, hus-band? What you rescue will immediately reveal what you treasure in your life.

Our treasures are what we hold dear - the things we consid-er essential to our survival, happiness and security. Our treasures often reveal our affections, ambitions and attractions. Unless our treasures are based on eternal realities, we stand the risk of losing everything.

Did you know that as Christians, where our treasure is will de-termine where our money or investments go? Did you know that money is one of the greatest treasures of most humans? Not only is money the only competitor that God has, but it is an impor-tant measuring rod which reveals where our priorities lie. Did you know that our church budgets and expenditures reveal where our real treasures lie?

Let me share with you a few things that reveal where our treasures lie today in the 21st-century Church:

1. **Building Projects and Cathedrals** - Without a doubt, church or fellowship buildings have served the Body of Christ a great deal in providing a place to worship the thrice Holy God, advance the course of the Kingdom, and minister to humani-ty. However, I believe, for many denominations, believers and church leaders today, it has become a symbol of status. Too often, we get the idea that many fellowships and leaders go to any length to erect church buildings to compete with another fellowship or leader, or just to show that "they have arrived!"

   Do we ever reflect on the idea that one of the most impor-tant reasons why we acquire buildings is for the harvest of souls? We must ask ourselves – is the amount of money invested in church buildings comparable to how much we invest in actual soul-winning endeavours?

   Remember, God has changed his address from a building to the hearts of men. A building, no matter it's worth or beauty is bound to pass away with the present system.

2. **Conferences, Anniversaries, Concerts, and Other Special Programmes** - You will be shocked and amazed at how much money churches spend every year on conferences, concerts and honoraria. What will amuse you the most is that a num-ber of these programmes don't even add to the advancement of God's Kingdom, righteousness and soul winning.

   I have watched for years how we invite special guest speak-ers, often from "God's own country", with all the pageantry and hype, yet for a whole week's programme, our speaker nev-er makes an altar call for sinners to repent. All he does is to entertain and mesmerize the saints!

3. **Evangelism and Missions** - How much we invest in our
    soul-winning endeavours is a clear indication of where our
    treasure lies. What percentage of our total budget do we al-
    locate to missionary endeavours to the unreached places
    who have never heard the Gospel in over 2,000 years? How
    much do we spend on outreaches to the prisons, hospitals,
    and brothels, and also on printing tracts and Bibles?

    All these are indicators of our priorities - where our true
    treasures lie. If our treasures are in Heaven or eternal realities,
    then we will invest more in every single activity that leads to
    soul winning and the expansion of the Kingdom of God.

    Did you know that Christians spend more money on dog
    food than on missions? Are you aware that statistics reveal
    that about 95% of American Christians' giving remains in
    the country for home-based ministry, 4.5% goes to outreach
    pro-grammes in already evangelised nations, and 0.5% only
    goes to the unreached people groups?

    There are a few Christian leaders who have inspired and
    challenged me more than the late missions' statesman -
    Oswald J. Smith, the one-time Senior Pastor of Peoples
    Church in Toronto, Canada. In his monumental work, The
    Cry of the World, he presented how his church gave both to
    home and foreign missions between 1933 and 1963. Without
    exception, throughout these 30 years, the church, every year,
    gave far more for missions and soul winning than she spent
    at home. Let's reflect a little on these statistics:

The Peoples Church, Toronto

YEAR	HOME CHURCH ($)	MISSIONS ($)
1933	18,185	23,568
1934	19,822	27,181
1935	26,338	28,102
1937	26,338	30,615
1938	21,230	40,029
1940	22,871	46,435
1941	21,135	54,417
1942	23,144	60,279
1943	23,953	78,413
1944	31,806	117,723
1946	25,379	122,440
1947	28,786	138,394
1948	38,356	177,473
1949	37,215	180,878
1951	38,832	216,443
1952	52,811	228,960
1953	40,813	245,260
1954	39,778	280,423
1956	44,250	289,502
1958	45,549	298,316
1961	49,273	303,345
1963	63,067	329,240

Any lessons from the above statistics? I believe a lot! Every Bible-believing church that professes to be serious with the business of soul winning ought to follow in the footsteps of the People's Church. We cannot claim that soul winning is our number one priority and yet spend more on other things. This is an error!

CHAPTER 15

THE SUPERNATURAL DIMENSION
OF THE GREAT COMMISSION

"'Go ye' is as much a part of Christ's Gospel as 'come unto me'.
You are not even a Christian until you have honestly faced your
responsibility in regard to the carrying of the Gospel to the ends
of the earth."
– J. Stuart Holden

"The history of missions is the history of

answered prayers." – Samuel Marinus Zwemer

"Intercession remains the unrivaled master in fulfilling the Great

Commission." – David Shibley

Did you know that there is a supernatural dimension to the Great
Commission? In my study of the Great Commission passages, I
discovered that whenever Jesus gave us the commission to evangelise the world, it was followed by supernatural power. There is
a promise of supernatural endowment and manifestation.

Let us consider some scriptures:

1. "And when he had called unto him his twelve disciples, he gave

them power against unclean spirits, to cast them out, and to heal all manner of sickness and all manner of disease."
– Matthew 10:1

2. "But go rather to the lost sheep of the house of Israel."
– Matthew 10:6

3. "And as ye go, preach, saying, The kingdom of heaven is at hand."
– Matthew 10:7

4. "Heal the sick, cleanse the lepers, raise the dead, cast out devils: freely ye have received, freely give."
– Matthew 10:8

5. This is the Markan version of the Great Commission; notice the supernatural power and manifestation:

"And he said unto them, 'Go ye into all the world, and preach the gospel to every creature. He that believeth and is baptized shall be saved; but he that believeth not shall be damned. And these signs shall follow them that believe; In my name shall they cast out devils; they shall speak with new tongues; They shall take up serpents; and if they drink any deadly thing, it shall not hurt them; they shall lay hands on the sick, and they shall recover." – Mark 16:15-18
Did you notice what is supposed to accompany our ministry?

6. "Then he called his twelve disciples together, and gave them power and authority over all devils, and to cure diseases. And he sent them to preach the kingdom of God, and to heal the sick."
– Luke 9:1-2

7. "After these things the Lord appointed other seventy also, and sent them two and before his face into every city and place, whither he himself would come."
    – Luke 10:1

8. "And into whatsoever city ye enter, and they receive you, eat such things as are set before you: And heal the sick that are therein, and say unto them, The kingdom of God is come nigh unto you."
    – Luke 10:8-9

9. "And said unto them, Thus it is written, and thus it behoved Christ to suffer, and to rise from the dead the third day: And that repent-ance and remission of sins should be preached in his name among all nations, beginning at Jerusalem. And ye are witnesses of these things. And, behold, I send the promise of my Father upon you: but tarry ye in the city of Jerusalem, until ye be endued with power from on high."
    – Luke 24:46-49

10. "Then said Jesus to them again, 'Peace be unto you: as my Father hath sent me, even so send I you.' And when he had said this, he breathed on them, and saith unto them, 'Receive ye the Holy Ghost.'"
    – John 20:21-22

11. Let's consider what kind of ministry Paul had among the Corinthians:

    "And my speech and my preaching was not with enticing words of man's wisdom, but in demonstration of the Spirit and of power."
    – 1 Corinthians 12:4.

Can we compare our ministry today with that of Paul?

12. Let's consider another example of Paul's ministry when he got to Paphos:

> "And when they had gone through the isle unto Paphos, they found a certain sorcerer, a false prophet, a Jew, whose name was Barjesus: Which was with the deputy of the country, Sergius Paulus, a pru-dent man; who called for Barnabas and Saul, and desired to hear the word of God. But Elymas the sorcerer (for so is his name by interpretation) withstood them, seeking to turn away the deputy from the faith."
> – Acts 13:6-13

Paul's reaction was immediate (verses 9-11):

> "Then Saul, (who also is called Paul) filled with the Holy Ghost, set his eyes on him, And said, 'O full of all subtilty and all mischief, thou child of the devil, thou enemy of all righteousness, wilt thou not cease to pervert the right ways of the Lord? And now, behold, the hand of the Lord is upon thee, and thou shalt be blind, not seeing the sun for a season.' And immediately there fell on him a mist and a darkness; and he went about seeking some to lead him by the hand."

What then was the consequence? (verse 12):

> "Then the deputy, when he saw what was done, believed, being as-tonished at the doctrine of the Lord."

This was what the Lord meant when He remarked in John 4:48,

> "Then said Jesus unto him, Except ye see signs and wonders, ye will not believe."

No wonder Moses refused to go to Egypt to face Pharaoh until his words were backed with signs and wonders. Signs, miracles and wonders are meant to authenticate our words, they are meant to prove that we have been sent by a Supernatural God. Again in Acts 9:36-42, Dorcas or Tabitha, the woman full of good works, was raised from the dead in Joppa. What was the effect on the people? Many believed in the Lord (verse 42).

Today, the world is waiting for us to prove that we have been sent by a Living God. They are asking us to authenticate our ministry. However, a large percentage of our preaching and ministry is mere rhetoric and noise making. Have you watched crusade vide-os of John J. Lake, Reinhard Bonnke, Pastor Chris of Christ Em-bassy or Bishop Dag? Why do you think these men pack entire stadiums and some record attendance in excess of a million? Why is it that at his death, Reinhard Bonnke was said to have led about 79 million people to the Lord? It was because his preachings were backed by signs and wonders and mighty deeds.

Let us reflect on a few reasons why a lot of Christian leaders and believers don't experience signs and wonders even though Jesus promised us greater works:

1. **Doubt** – James 1:6-8 charges us to ask in faith, not doubting anything. For anyone who doubts is like the wave of the sea. Such a man will not receive anything from God.

2. **Our Reputation** - Too many of God's children are too concerned about their reputation. We entertain thoughts such as 'What will happen if we pray and people don't get healed?' We should be dead to the world and shouldn't care about our reputation.

3. **Price** - There is a price tag attached to signs and wonders. This kind cannot go except by prayer and fasting. Ask anyone who operates in the supernatural and they will testify of the price they have paid.

CHAPTER 16

CALLED FOR SUCH A TIME AS THIS

"The   Great Commission is still the Missions
Statement of the Church."
– Dallas Willard

"There is no higher calling or greater privilege
known to man than being involved in helping fulfil
the Great Commission." – Billy Bright

"The   Great Commission will not be fulfilled with
our spare time or spare money."
– David Kim

"And Mordecai told them to answer Esther: "Do not think in your heart that you will escape in the king's palace any more than all the other Jews. For if you remain completely silent at this time, relief and deliverance will arise for the Jews from another place, but you and your father's house will perish. Yet who knows whether you have come to the kingdom for such a time as this?"
– Esther 4:13-14 (NKJV)

The Book of Esther is such an interesting book in many respects. The first thing worth mentioning about this book is that throughout, you never find the word God, yet you see Him operating behind the scenes. This goes to confirm that history is God's story; there is nothing that happens on earth outside of His control and jurisdiction. When you read in-between the story of Esther, you will notice the workings of God.

According to Psalm 75:6-7 (KJV):

"For promotion [cometh] neither from the east, nor from the west, nor from the south. But God [is] the judge: he putteth down one, and setteth up another."

A few interesting things from this book that we can learn are:

1) Queen Vashti – The King Ahasuerus made a feast for his offi-cials and subjects to display his splendour and majesty at the pal-ace of Shushan. When the heart of the king was merry with wine, he called for the queen to come and show her beauty. However, she refused - a thing unheard of. Later on, he sought the counsel of his officials and it was decided that Vashti be removed and re-placed with someone else.

2) The Search for a Replacement Begins – Many virgins were chosen to go through preparations, after which they were to ap-pear before the king for one night. Whoever he was pleased with would replace Queen Vashti.

3) God never calls the qualified but He qualifies the called. The Bible records that He calls the foolish things of this world so that no man can boast in his sight. There was a young orphan girl in the kingdom. She was a foreigner and, therefore, not qualified, but her uncle, Mordecai, encouraged her to contest anyway.

4) The Favour of God - We see that everywhere Esther turned, she experienced the favour of God. With the beauty preparations, she was given far more than she needed and also above her com-petitors. This situation would seem to resonate with many of us, at least with me. He didn't choose us because we were wise, nor from noble backgrounds, nor mighty. He chose us who were weak and foolish, so that He may confound the strong and the wise.

5) Haman's Plot - Another dimension of this story, critical to this chapter, was the plot of Haman. He hated Mordecai for no just reason and thus extended his hatred to the Jews in the Empire. Through several plotting and manipulations, he chose a date, made a huge deposit into the king's treasury and got the king to sign and seal a declaration to destroy and annihilate the Jews on a certain date.

6) The Fate of the Jews - After Mordecai learnt all that had hap-pened, he tore his clothes and put on sackcloth, and went into the midst of the city, crying out with a loud and bitter voice. He went as far as the front of the king's gate, for no one might enter the king's gate clothed with sackcloth. There was great mourning amongst the Jews, with fasting, weeping and wailing, and many lay in sackcloth and ashes.

So Esther's maids and eunuchs told her what was happening to her people and she became deeply distressed. Then she sent garments to clothe Mordecai and to take his sackcloth away from him, but he would not accept them. Esther then sent some of her attendants to find out what was wrong with her uncle, Mordecai. So Hathach went out to Mordecai to learn what was the matter. Mordecai informed him of all that Haman planned to do to de-stroy the Jews. He also gave him a copy of the written decree for their destruction to show to Esther so that she could go before the king to plead with Him to abort the intent of Haman.

Esther's reply to Mordecai was:

> "All the king's servants and the people of the king's provinces know that any man or woman who goes into the inner court to the king, who has not been called, he has but one law: put all to death, except the one to whom the king holds out the golden scepter, that he may live. Yet I myself have not been called to go in to the king these thirty days." So they told Mordecai Esther's words." – Esther 4:11-12 (NKJV)

The response of Mordecai to Esther is the core message that the Holy Spirit wants to highlight to us -

> "Do not think in your heart that you will escape in the king's palace any more than all the other Jews. For if you remain completely silent at this time, relief and deliverance will arise for the Jews from another place, but you and your father's house will perish. Yet who knows whether you have come to the kingdom for such a time as this." - Esther 4:13-14 (NKJV)

I am convinced that where you are presently, socially, economically or politically is a set up by the Holy Spirit. God has raised, trained and positioned you for the benefit and salvation of many! There-fore, it is time to shake yourself out of the dust of indifference and apathy, and step into your divine calling and assignment. For do you know whether you have been called for such a time as this?

CHAPTER 17

THE BATON HAS BEEN HANDED TO YOU

"Every Christian is either a missionary or an impostor."
– Charles Spurgeon

"If we understand what lies ahead for those who do not know Christ, there will be a sense of urgency in our witness." – David Jeremiah

"Love your fellowmen, and cry about them if you cannot bring them to Christ. If you cannot save them, you can weep over them. If you cannot give them a drop of cold water in hell, you can give them your heart's tears while they are still in this body."
- Charles Spurgeon

"This is the genealogy of Jesus the Messiah the son of David, the son of Abraham: Abraham was the father of Isaac, Isaac the father of Jacob, Jacob the father of Judah and his brothers…" – Matthew 1:1-17 (NIV):

"Thus there were fourteen generations in all from Abraham to David, fourteen from David to the exile to Babylon, and fourteen from the exile to the Messiah."
– Verse 17

"Then he said, "I am the God of your father, the God of Abraham, the God of Isaac and the God of Jacob." – Exodus 3:6 (NIV)

This message is to all believers across the globe. It is to all men and women, boys and girls, young and old. It is to those in the Doma gifts as well as the foot soldiers. The call is to all those in the seven spheres of society - 1) government and politics 2) economy 3) education 4) religion 5) family 6) media, and finally, 7) entertainment (sports, art, fashion etc.) - those whose assignment and ministry is to conquer these seven mountains.

I have discovered a very important truth from God's Word - God is a God of generations. He calls different generations and allots to them a unique assignment to further His programme here on earth. Like the Olympic relay teams, every generation has a unique contribution to make towards the propagation of the Gospel and the advancement of the Kingdom of God.

"Do you not know that in a race, all the runners run."

–1 Corinthians 9:24 (NIV)

"Therefore, since we are surrounded by such a great cloud of witnesses, let us throw off everything that hinders and the sin that so easily en-tangles. And let us run with perseverance the race marked out for us." – Hebrews 12:1 (NIV)

There is a race that is set before you and me. There's a reason why God has sent us to our generation.

The first member of our team - the Early or first-century Church, took off with such an amazing speed, beating all competition hands down, putting in all they had and thus giving a huge advantage to those they handed the baton to. Read Church history and you will appreciate what a small and mostly uneducated bunch did, turning major cities upside down for Jesus. Such was the impact of the Early Church, with such team members like Peter, James, John, Philip, and the chief of all apostles - Paul. In my estimation, their outstanding feat has not been replicated by succeeding generations.

Saint Patrick (431 AD – 461 AD) - After the Apostles' era, another relay team member of a different generation who is worthy of note is Saint Patrick, the 5th-century founder of the Irish Catholic Church, a formidable missionary church.

Ramon Llull (1232 - 1315) - He took the baton and represented another team and generation in God's economy. How did he run his race? By being a missionary to the Muslims. He learnt Ar-abic and promoted serious apologetics. He evangelised in North Africa and eventually died a martyr.

David Brainerd (1718 -1747) - He was an American missionary to the Native Americans and represents the team of the 18th century. He had a very fruitful ministry, in his rather short life, to the Delaware Indians in New Jersey. Even though his life was very short, the exploits of his life, contained in his biography written by Jonathan Edward, soon became an inspiration to many - in-cluding the saintly John Wesley, Henry Martyn, William Carey and Jim Elliot.

Count Nicolaus Ludwig Von Zinzendorf (1700 - 1760) - He was one of the team members of the 18th century and one of the greatest inspiration of all time, as far as the missionary enterprise is concerned. He led the Moravians who have had the longest prayer movement in history; 24-hours unbroken prayers that last-ed over 100 years. His challenge to his community was to win for the Lamb the reward of His sacrifice. As a result of his inspiration and their prayers, many of them sold themselves as slaves to travel to different parts of the world - just to share the Gospel to unreached places. John Wesley's conversion was traceable to the activities of the Moravians.

William Carey (1761 - 1834) - Often referred to as the father of modern missions, William Carey was a Baptist Minister, a mis-sionary, Bible translator, soul reformer and cultural anthropologist. He began his work in India, founding schools for poor children. His work and writings are responsible for the founding of the Baptist Missionary Society, whose reach covers 40 countries. He translated the Bible into dozens of Indian dialects and founded a missions' college to train ministers. He is credited with the famous quote that has inspired many - "Expect great things from God. Attempt great things for God."

Mary Slessor (1848 – 1915) - Commonly known as the Queen of Calabar because of her missionary journey to Calabar, Nige-ria. She was also a social reformer and judge. Before she got to Calabar, twins were considered to be children of the devil, and as such, thrown into the forest to die. Well, not on her watch! Mary Slessor fought against this barbaric act and made Jesus famous in her generation. She's now in the grandstands cheering us on to bring in the great harvest!

Suffice to say, there are many more generals who have left their footprints in the sands of time, namely George Mueller and his activities with orphaned children, Jim and Elizabeth Elliot, Da-vid Livingstone - a medical missionary who spent most of his life in Africa. His love for Africa is exemplified in the sense that when he died, his heart was removed and buried under a tree in Africa before his body was transported to Britain. Others include Hudson Taylor, a missionary to China; Amy Carmichael, an Irish missionary to India; and more recently, Eric Liddell, Dr Billy

Graham and Reinhard Bonnke.

Now the baton has been handed over to us - no generation since the Early Church has been better equipped, more enriched with greater privileges, more equipment and resources, but also with a heightened responsibility to complete the Great Commission Mandate.

All the preceding generations, who are our cloud of witnesses, are cheering us on to forge ahead and complete the Great Commission. However, many of them are in tears, as it seems that most of what was gained from them has been lost by our generation because of apathy, lukewarmness, indifference, carnality, divisions and so many distractions.

Friend, do you know that the baton has been handed over to you? This is a once-in-a-lifetime opportunity to prove your love for Jesus. You will never have a second opportunity. Time is racing against us! Paul was so successful because he considered ministry as a trust.

> "According to the glorious gospel of the blessed God, which was committed to my trust."
> – 1 Timothy 1:11 (KJV)

Guard the treasure entrusted to you with the help of the Holy Spirit. Would you arise, take your place and make your mark in your generation?

SPECIAL INVITATION

I am totally convinced that this book did not come into your hands by sheer coincidence – it was orchestrated by God!

If you have never at any point in time opened up your heart to receive Jesus and accept Him as your Lord and Personal Saviour – you can do so right now!

Why not say this short prayer?

Dear Jesus! Thank you for dying on the Cross for me. I believe you died and God raised you up on the third day for my salvation. I accept you today as my Lord and Personal Saviour.

Thank you for saving me! Amen!

OTHER TITLES BY THE AUTHOR

If this book has touched you, why not place an order for other books!

1. Great Britain Has Fallen
2. Awake Great Britain
3. Awake Canada
4. Pastoral Abuse
5. The Call of God
6. The Parable of the Pound
7. Dreams: From Conception to Reality
8. Fulfilling Your Destiny
9. Occupying Vacant Position
10. The Wilderness Experience
11. Overcoming the Enemy Within
12. Great Men and Women who made Great Britain Great
13. Benefits of Affliction
14. You Can Plead your Case
15. The 401 Prophet
16. Barrenness; Its Curses and Cures
17. Finishing Your Assignment In Life
18. Growing Into the Image of Christ
19. Finishing The Great Commission
20. The Effective Follow Up Ministry

CONTACT DETAILS

World Harvest Christian Centre
7 Enmore Road
South Norwood
London
SE25 5NQ
United Kingdom

Email: admin@worldharvest.org.uk & info@walebabatunde.com
website: www.worldharvest.org.uk & www.walebabatunde.com
Facebook: @whcclondon, @PastorWaleBabatunde
Twitter: @whcc_london, @PastorWale_
YouTube: PastorWale
Instagram: PastorWale_
Soundcloud: PastorWale_